LOOK AT THE FUTURE AND LAUGH!

ANNA R. HERNANDEZ

LOOK AT THE FUTURE AND LAUGH!

ANNA R. HERNANDEZ

Copyright © 2020
All Rights Reserved

Look at the Future And Laugh, 2nd Edition

This book may not be reproduced, transmitted, or stored in whole or in part by any means, including graphics, electronic, or mechanical without the express written consent of the publisher except in the case of brief quotations embodied in critical articles and reviews.

Eternalimpact@live.com
989-737-1334
Facebook: Eternal Impact Media Ministries

All scripture quoted in this book is from the King James Authorized Version of the Bible.

ISBN: 9798609330581

TABLE OF CONTENTS

Acknowledgment...................................Page 2
Introduction...Page 5

Chapter 1
    Victorious View................................ Page 7

Chapter 2
    No Discounts...................................Page 19

Chapter 3
    Seeing Beyond Now.................................Page 45

Chapter 4
    Losing the Rearview Mirror ....Page 63

Chapter 5
    Suddenly.......................................Page 77

Chapter 6
    From Venom to Virtue.............................Page 93

Chapter 7
    Finding Hope..............................;........Page 105

Chapter 8
    Releasing the Law of Kindness...............Page 125

Chapter 9
    Experience Brings Hope ....Page 139

Chapter 10
    Call Her Blessed.................................Page 145

Epilogue..Page 153
About the Author...................................Page 154

Acknowledgment

I would like to thank the many wonderful people God has placed in my life that helped me complete this book. During the writing of this book, I have reflected on the positive influence that each one of you has made in my life and how your friendship has drawn me closer to my father, God. I want to acknowledge:

- My husband George. Thank you for helping me to stir up the gift inside of me. For the past 25 years, you have stood alongside me and cheered me on. You helped me keep up with our everyday activities so that I could find time to write or study. I love you George and I am so proud to be your wife.
- Our daughter, Adina. You have brought us so much joy. We prayed for a child and God granted us such a beautiful daughter. You have always encouraged me, and you so faithfully served the Lord alongside us as we've spent many weekends on the road traveling to share the Good news to others. We love you.
- Dr. Joseph Rodriguez and Rev. Eva Rodriguez, thank you for being my spiritual parents. The daily example you set before me has challenged me to seek more of God and gain a greater understanding of His Word. Thank you for being there for us. You transformed our marriage by teaching us to walk by faith. We will never be the same.
- Mom and Dad, thank you for raising me in the things of the Lord. Your passion to bring others to Christ has been such an example to me. It has been amazing to see how both of you have faced the adversities of life and yet continued to point others to Jesus. I love you both.

- Casandra Miller, my friend, and encourager. Thank you for all you did to edit the book and help me bring about God's word with simplicity and clarity.
- Jennifer Borchard, my friend, and proof-reader. We've shared an office, watched our daughters grow and now you helped me share the Good news of the gospel. Thank you.
- Jeri Darby, my writing coach. Thank you for being a friend, source of encouragement and accountability partner. You've helped me cross the "finish line" of this second release.
- Chelsea Castillo, my "daughter" and graphic artist. You are like a daughter to me and your "Uncle George" It has been a pleasure watching you grow. Thank you for sharing your artistic talents and creativity with God's people.
- Mick McArt, my friend and fellow self-publisher. Thank you for encouraging me to start writing so many years ago. Thank you for navigating me through this publishing process.
- Shirley Witteborg, My 11th grade English teacher. I will always remember our "talks" and how you encouraged me to pursue writing. I didn't realize it then, but it was God speaking through you. I'm so glad we bumped into each other 30 years later.

Introduction

This book was written from a state of brokenness. We were dealing with infertility and there was nothing I could do to change our situation. I had to find a way to move on with my life with a broken heart and shattered dreams. The multiple miscarriages were painful, and I could not ignore, deny or bury my grief with work or other activity. I was at a point in my life where I was no longer "in control" and nothing made sense. The situation was unfair, and I was angry. There was only one source of comfort and that was God.

My soul was traumatized and broken. It needed to be healed. It was out of sheer desperation, that I began to read the Bible searching for answers. I have since realized that emotional healing is also a process. If you have experienced any type of loss whether it is a child, loved one, job, marriage or you are facing financial problems, these storms of life have hurt your soul. Your soul is the part of you that thinks, feels and lives life. This book was written to help restore your soul.

The healing process requires rest for you to regain your strength. You must slow down and allow God to speak to you through the pages of this book. His greatest desire for you is to understand that you are not alone. This situation you are going through is not the end of your story. It is one of life's let downs, but it does not have the final say in who you are. You can find hope amid the darkness.

As with the body, time and rest bring restoration. To regain full use of a broken part, physical therapy and rehabilitation are often required. The same is true with your soul. It will take discipline to study the lives of people who have suffered many of the same things we still experience today. You will need to allow the Holy Spirit, God's power to change your thinking. It is only by changing your mindset that you will find peace and hope. It is His peace that will bring you to a place where you can *Look At The Future and Laugh*. You will not laugh at the circumstance, but you will rejoice knowing brighter days are ahead of you.

Chapter 1

Victorious View

*Strength and honor are her clothing;
and She shall rejoice in time to come.
Proverbs 31:25*

WHEN MANY PEOPLE look at the future all they see is loss, desperation, emptiness, and heartache. They turn on the evening news and are constantly bombarded with stories about wars, terrorism threats, economic instability, and rampant violence. It seems like violence is ripping across the U.S. and not even rural small towns are shielded from its painful destruction. We are living in a time when every sector of our society is undergoing rapid change. The news of constant change and uncertainty is leaving many people fearful about the future. Yes, we are living in very difficult times but today, I want to help you find a reason to hope and believe for a victorious future. No matter what obstacle or difficulty you are facing right now, there is hope. You can find the strength you need to look forward to tomorrow. You can rebuild your life and instead of dreading the unknown, you can get excited about the possibilities. This year can be one of the best years of your life. Your future can be one filled with love, joy, and peace but the positive changes will have to start inside of you. You must be able to look at your future-and laugh.

Maybe you're reading this book right now and are asking yourself, *"How can I look at the future and laugh if I've just faced a tragic situation and my life will never be the same?"* How do you look at the future and laugh when you've given everything to build a career but now the company is bankrupt, or they've eliminated your position? You realize that during the process of building a career you've lost your marriage, your children, and you will never get back the time you devoted to that company. How do you look at the future and laugh when you've been diagnosed with an incurable disease for which there is no cure? How do you look at the future and laugh when the person you married walks out on you and leaves you alone to raise the children? How do you look at the future and laugh when you've watched drug or alcohol addiction take total control of a loved one?

You've tried to intervene, but they pushed you away and now they steal, lie, and to get their next fix, they take anything they can from you. All of these situations are painful and the lives of the people who have experienced them will never be the same. But there is hope. It is not a natural hope; rather, a true hope which comes from God once we realize that there is an eternal perspective on what we go through. What we see here is natural. The Bible says that what is seen is temporal but what is unseen is eternal. 2 Corinthians 4:18 Therefore, when the hardships come to each of us, we must find an eternal or supernatural anchor to rest upon. ***"Which hope we have an anchor of the soul, both sure and stedfast, and which entereth into at within the veil;" Hebrews 6:19***

When we face circumstances that we don't understand and seem unfair, we must learn to trust and believe that God has an eternal perspective. He offers everyone a true source of hope and strength that enables us to live full and happy lives, instead of merely existing, after the disappointments and losses of life. I know from my personal experience what it is to wonder if God really cares about every area of our lives.

For many years, I struggled with my relationship with God. You see, my deepest desire at one point in life was to have a child. My husband and I were married in the fall of 1991, and as newlyweds, we were focused on our careers. In a time when we thought we were "ready", we decided it was time to start a family. Everything seemed to be going along perfectly and according to our plan, except for one thing: after five years of trying to conceive a child, there was still no baby. We went from one fertility doctor who told us there was nothing to worry about, to another. No one could find a reason why we couldn't have children. Suddenly, we faced a situation that we couldn't control and after several miscarriages, we were beginning to lose hope of ever holding a child of our own. Month by month, the perfect "family" picture of three children, a dog, and a cat was slowly being shattered. I began to accept this situation as "God's will" and turned to my work as a shelter from the pain and emptiness I felt.

People tried to comfort me and even though I listened to what they said, my heart was resentful. I questioned whether anyone truly understood my pain. How could I get past infertility and just go on with my life? It seemed like the harder we tried to conceive a child the more that dream eluded us. As a result of this disappointment, I began to just exist. I lost hope and felt bewildered by the unanswered question that gnawed at my thoughts every day, *"Why, God, why?"* Things just didn't seem "fair".

We were married, going to church, had a home, and was truly in love with each other. Yet, we couldn't have a baby. I chose to hide my pain behind a wall of self-effort to achieve worldly success. I was alive but had no joy for life. I could see, but I did not have a true vision for my life, because I had allowed the disappointment of infertility to blind me to the blessings that were still in front of me. During this period of my life, it was especially difficult to attend Mother's Day services and listen to the preacher's sermon about the "Proverbs 31" woman. Proverbs 31:10-3110 states:

"Who can find a virtuous wife? For her worth is far above rubies. The heart of her husband doth safely trust in her, so he shall not need spoil. She will do him good and not evil all the days of her life. She seeketh wool, and flax, and worketh willingly with her hands. She is like the merchants' ship, she bringeth her food from afar. She riseth also while it is yet night, and giveth meat to her household, and a portion to her maidens. She considereth a field, ad buyeth it: with the fruit of her hands she planteth a vineyard. She girdeth her loins with strength and strengthens her arms. She perceiveth that her merchandise is good, and her candle goeth not out by night. She layeth her hands to the spindle, and her hands hold the distaff. She stretcheth out her hand to the poor, yea, she reacheth forth hands to the needy. She is not afraid of snow for her household: for all her household is clothed with scarlet. She maketh herself coverings of tapestry; her clothing is silk and purple. Her husband is known in the gates, when he sitteth among the elders of the land. She maketh fine linen, and selleth it: and deliverth girdles unto the merchant. Strength and honor are her clothing; and She shall rejoice in time to

come. She openeth her mouth with wisdom, and on her tongue is the law of kindness. She well to the ways of her household, and eateth not the bread of idleness. Her children rise up and call her blessed; her husband also, and he praiseth her. Many daughters have done virtuously, but thou excellest them all. Favor is deceitful and beauty is vain, but a woman that feareth the Lord, she shall be praised. Give her of the fruit of her hands, and let her own works praise her in the gates."

This portion of scripture describes a biblical wife completely devoted to her husband, children, and God. Whenever anyone taught on this Virtuous Woman, I felt condemned and inadequate. The way she was portrayed made me think that she was perfect. I wondered if she was even a real woman or just a role model that I could never live up to, especially given the fact that I could not have children. I would leave the church wondering if this woman was only defined by what she did at home with the children and with her husband. I knew that how we lived our everyday lives was important to God, but I struggled between my desire to draw closer to Him and my desire to fulfill my daily responsibilities. It looked like this Proverbs 31 woman was too perfect and I struggled to maintain a balance between my work schedule, volunteer commitments, household duties, and my desire to enjoy life. It seemed like there just weren't enough hours in the day to get it all done. I wanted off the fast-paced treadmill called life. It was as if a war raged inside of me. I worried about whether my house was spotless, and I stressed about the laundry getting washed. I worried about what the neighbors would think if my landscaping didn't look good and my flower beds weren't in full bloom throughout the summer. Then, I would feel guilty because I wasn't studying or reading the Bible as I desired to do. I'd go to church, but while I was there, it was difficult for me to get anything from the messages because my mind was so consumed by things, events, and my never-ending To-Do list.

For years, this Virtuous Woman described in Proverbs 31 annoyed me. I wondered if God really expected us to rise before dawn to fix breakfast for the family, work with our hands all day long, show up to PTA meetings, be in the choir, head the hospitality committee at church, be the perfect wife, and tend to aging parents, all while maintaining ourselves full of love, joy, peace, and kindness all the time? Deep in my heart, I knew there had to be more to the virtuous woman than just doing good things to please God. I was searching to define what it meant to be a virtuous woman? How could I become a virtuous woman? I asked God to help me understand her. I wanted to know more about her because there was more to her than simply being a nice lady.

One day, I thought of an old Spanish song that we used to sing in church. It was based upon one of Jesus' miracles. He healed a woman who the Bible describes as having a flow of blood for twelve years. *"And Jesus, immediately knowing in himself that virtue had gone out of him, turned him about in the press, and said, Who touched my clothes?" Mark 5:30* All of a sudden, my eyes were opened, and I saw it-the root word of virtue was used in this verse, but a different application. Webster's Dictionary defines virtuous as *A particular moral excellence; 2 beneficial quality or power of a thing; 3 a capacity to act: potency c: the ability or capacity to achieve or bring about a particular result.* In Mark 5:30. Jesus felt that virtue, or power, had been released from His body and in that instant, somebody's life was changed. The woman that

Jesus healed was forbidden by her society to interact with anyone because the Jewish laws called her "unclean". She had spent everything she had going from doctor to doctor looking for a cure. During those twelve years, the pain in her body was compounded by the pain of rejection from society and the loss of the life that she once knew. She agonized over the fact that no one could change her situation. If she were married, I imagine that she longed for the intimacy and security she drew from her husband.

As the years progressed, the disease would have strained her marriage, because the religious laws of her society prohibited any sexual contact with her husband. We know that she was weak and fragile, so she could no longer work and was dependent on others for everything. All that she had left were the memories of what "used to be". She had no hope and only a cloud of despair and grief lingered around her. That was her condition until the day she heard about Jesus. It seemed as though out of nowhere, like a ray of light the possibility of change sprang up in her heart.

She heard that Jesus had the power to heal any disease and she was determined to take whatever action was necessary to simply touch the hem of His robe. She realized that if she wanted to get better, she would have to seek Jesus, the Healer. She would find the strength to press through the mob that swarmed around Him. This would be risky because she faced the possibility of condemnation from the religious leaders, who could call for her to be stoned because she was appearing in public in an "unclean" state. Yet, in spite of these obstacles, this woman found hope that grew into faith as she kept saying to herself, "If I can touch Jesus, I will be made well." This Virtuous Woman tapped into the supernatural Law of Faith. In Romans 10:17 the scriptures tell us: **"So then faith cometh by hearing,**

and hearing by the word of God." This woman heard that Jesus was healing all sorts of people. As she heard that the lame was walking and blind eyes were opened, hope sprung up in her heart. She kept hearing until, finally, that hope grew into faith. Then, faith prompted her into action. The second part of the Law of Faith she applied is found in Romans 4:17: ***"Before him whom he believed even God, who quickeneth the dead, and calleth those things which be not as though they were."***

As she made her way through the crowd, she was declaring, or calling, herself well. While she stepped out toward Jesus, she was releasing faith-filled words into the spiritual realm. Those words pleased God. *"I know if I can touch Jesus, I will be made well."* As she spoke, faith grew more and more, because she was calling those things which be not as though they were. Her life was a wreck. She didn't have a penny to her name. In the natural, there was nothing left for her to try, but faith motivated her to push everybody and everything aside as she made her way to Jesus.

I imagine she kept seeing a mental picture of her future reunited with her family. She was laughing on the inside because her eyes were fixed on getting to Jesus. She had replaced every thought of sickness and disease with an image of health and strength. As she made her way to Jesus, she was mentally taking off the smelly unclean rags and putting on garments of strength and dignity. Everyone might have been looking at a sickly woman in the natural, but they could not see how the power of her faith was tapping into the virtue of Jesus. What is even more beautiful, is Jesus' response to her when she steps forward and tells Him that she was the one who touched him. ***"Daughter, thy faith hath made thee whole; go in peace, and be whole of thy plague." Mark 5:34***

Jesus not only healed her body because the wholeness that He was speaking about was greater than just physical healing. It meant a restoration of all that she had lost. Her body was instantly healed, her marriage would be restored, she would be reunited with her family and accepted back into society. Her faith had made her whole. This depleted woman painted a portrait of a virtuous woman. I finally understood that a virtuous woman comprehends that when she trusts the power of God within her, she has the ability of Almighty God to bring about a particular result.

A virtuous woman can find light in the darkest places, by speaking the Word of God. She can pray for her loved ones, no matter how far away they are because there is no distance in the spirit realm. She can be a peacemaker where there is turmoil and show love in a world full of hate. Does that mean that she will never face tests or trials? No; things will not always be perfect. We will all be challenged during our lifetime. However, when trials arise, we can stand confidently on God's Word, knowing that He is for us. When you choose to follow His ways and are determined not to do what everyone else is doing, you become rare. We can walk in moral excellence in this world, not because of our strength or merits, but because of the power of Jesus inside of us. We can learn to trust God, regardless of what we see with our natural temporal eyes.

Please understand, I'm not a licensed psychologist or therapist, so this book isn't intended to be a motivational self-help manual with seven easy steps to follow to erase all the pain in your life. But what I can honestly say, is that I am a happy woman, who, by studying God's Word and examining the lives of biblical women, was able to get beyond life's letdowns and laugh again.

Your struggle is not unique. Disappointments and heartaches come to all of us in many different ways. It can be a divorce you never saw coming, the loss of a loved one, the emptiness of infertility, or an empty nest. It is my hope that through the stories in this book you will see that regardless of what your situation is, you can rebuild your life. It may not be the way it was before, but you can laugh once more. There is hope if you are willing to look beyond this natural realm.

Throughout this book, we are going to explore the lives of men and women, so that we can draw from the virtuous and spiritual principles that they exemplify. Principles that I will include are:

No Discounts – A review of the life of Esther, an orphan girl who ascends to power and uses her influence to save a nation.

Seeing Beyond Now – A study of the life of Sarah, a 90-year-old woman who faced years of infertility and by faith received the strength to conceive a miracle son.

Losing the Rearview Mirror – Looking at the life of a nameless woman whose desperate efforts to cling to her possessions caused her to lose what mattered most.

Suddenly – Learning how a widow saved her sons from slavery by tapping into God's financial system.

Venom to Virtue –Discover how Rahab broke free from the shackles of prostitution and secured a place in the lineage of the Lord Jesus Christ.

Finding Hope – Reviewing the life of Naomi, a widow who in the midst of the grief was able to see God intervening in the life of Ruth and mentored her so that she could start a new life.

Releasing the Law of Kindness – King David remembers the covenant he made with his friend Jonathan and restores all that was taken from an orphan son.

Experience Brings Hope –Developing a relationship with God through the experiences of life.

Call Her Blessed - Celebrating the courageous decision of a young woman in crisis.

Chapter 2

No Discounts

*Who can find a virtuous woman? for her price
is far above rubies.
Proverbs 31:10*

DO YOU KNOW WHY waterfront property is so expensive? It is because everyone wants to enjoy the beauty of the calm waters, but there is a limited supply available. God isn't making any more natural lakes or ocean beaches. No two properties are exactly alike. The value of the land is determined by its location. It is the economic law of Supply and Demand in operation; as the availability of land decreases and the number of buyers willing to purchase it grows, the price will increase. However, if that same land is later found to be contaminated by pollution, then the number of buyers interested in purchasing that property decreases and its value also decreases. Unlike property you must understand that as a Virtuous Woman, your worth cannot be calculated in natural terms because you are made in the image of God; you are a duplicate of His likeness. According to Psalms 139:14: ***"I will praise thee; for I am***

fearfully and wonderfully made; marvelous are thy works; and that my soul knoweth right well."

God saw the human race in its worst depravity and yet He wanted to redeem us because we are priceless to Him. . He sent the very best that He had to free us from the bondage of sin. He sent Jesus, His only begotten Son. There was nothing of any higher worth that could redeem us. God wanted to pay this price to free His precious children from the bonds of sin. He wanted us to have His nature inside of us. He wanted to give us His name, children of the Most High God. The problem that we face is that we underestimate our value and are willing to accept discounts. Webster defines a discount as ***A reduction made from the gross amount or value of something.***

When you discount and fail to cultivate your talents and abilities to their fullest potential, you begin to feel bored, frustrated, and dissatisfied. Have you ever looked at your life and wondered if where you are right now is "it"? Is this as good as it gets, or have I missed my life's purpose? Have you asked, does everyone really have a purpose or do people merely exist? Maybe you've never really thought about it because you've been so busy earning a living and just trying to keep up with the constant demands of your job and life responsibilities. You get up every day and go through your usual routine- maybe work, school, or your duties at home and it's so mundane, the same thing over and over again, month after month, year after year.

Maybe you find yourself facing the consequences of a poor decision that was based on a bad relationship or an empty promise. You had dreams and aspirations, but before you knew it, "life happened." Life's circumstances caught up with you and those dreams of a life filled with happiness, fun, and excitement are unfulfilled and with each passing day, it seems like all you do is exist. You realize that "the discount" has robbed you of your destiny and purpose. How does that happen? At what point did you quit believing in your dreams and accept the lies that your enemy, the devil tells you? It is because he plants lying thoughts in your mind. His lies aim to destroy your potential. Jesus stated, ***"The thief, cometh not but for to steal, and to kill, and to destroy:" John 10:10***

He wants to destroy your life and dreams. This is why he speaks lies such as "It's too late to change your past. You'll never amount to anything! You can't achieve that, no one in our family has ever done that before." Before you realize it, you internalize these lies into your thinking and they breed self-doubt. With flashes of defeat, this self-doubt bombards your vision for a bright future. These thoughts paralyze you from ever imagining a better future. If you allow it, your mind replays every time you tried something new and failed. Those thoughts of self-defeat have crushed the aspirations of many authors, entrepreneurs, ministers, entertainers, and countless other victims. Before you realize it, slowly, day-by-day, year-by-year the dream inside of you dies. You're always in motion, but never really getting anywhere.

I remember the first time I was challenged to take an honest look at my life and identify areas where I had accepted a discount. It was on February 19, 2005, at a Leading Ladies class that my mentor, Reverend Eva Rodriguez, taught. She explained that in order for us to have the God-kind of life here on earth, a victorious life, we must make changes to get rid of a "discount" mentality. We have the responsibility to align our minds with what God says about us. Before you were even born, God declared that His thoughts were thoughts of peace, and not evil, to bring you to your destiny.

"For I know the thoughts that I think toward you, saith the Lord, thoughts of peace, and not evil, to give you an expected end." Jeremiah 29:11 *"And be not conformed to this world: but be ye transformed by the renewing of your mind, that ye may prove what is that good, and acceptable, and perfect, will of God."* **Romans 12:21**

You can find His will for your life in any situation by studying the Bible and allowing His word to cleanse your thinking. You must remove the misinformation that the enemy has planted over many years, by consistently meditating on the Word of God. This type of thinking; fear, doubt, mistrust, anger, resentfulness, poverty, and even worry, all must be brought under subjection. These thoughts will only yield to one thing, the Word of God. The Bible states that God has called us to glory and virtue. We've already defined virtue, as the power and the ability to bring about change. *"**According as his divine power hath given unto us all things that pertain unto life and godliness, through the knowledge of him that hath called us to glory and virtue."* 2 Peter 1:3**

If we are going to please the Father, we cannot yield to our old way of thinking. We must renew our minds with the Word of God so that we begin to change our perspective. Did you notice what 2 Peter 1:3 says? God has already provided ***all things*** that pertain to life and godliness. If God has declared that He has an expected end for your life, then trust His Word; which states that we already have everything we need to obtain a successful future. If you are to become a virtuous woman, you must allow God's Word to wash away the painful memories of your past. You cannot carry the baggage of my past mistakes, hurts, disappointments, and wrong choices into your future. You cannot allow thoughts of defeat, bitterness, anger, and worry to consume you. You must decide to master your way of thinking. God places the responsibility of directing your life on you because He gave you a free-will. The problem many of us face is that we aren't willing to go through the process of renewing our mind and we want everything instantly. We are reluctant to wait on God's timing to obtain the best for our lives.

Let's go back to our lakefront property example. Imagine owning a cottage along a beautiful lake that has been in your family for generations. It is worth $3 million, but you decide to sell it because you are facing financial difficulties. You list the property on the market at full price and after waiting five days you start getting desperate and are tired of waiting for a buyer, so you decide to mark it down. The price is reduced from $3 million to $1 million and, almost instantly, the property sells within one hour of posting the new price. Why did it sell so fast? It sold quickly because it was a deal. You were willing to accept less than what it was worth, just to make the deal happen. Even though you knew it was worth more than $1 million you lowered your expectation and settled for less than what it was worth. How many times in our lives have we been willing to accept a discount, just because we could not wait for the right thing to happen?

Often, we enter into relationships that we know aren't right for us, because we don't want to be alone. We take jobs that are below our skill set because we are afraid that we won't get another offer. We stay stuck in jobs where we are miserable because we are afraid of venturing out to start that new business. In many instances, we discount our abilities, or we downplay them, in false humility. When people compliment us on something we've done well, we laugh and say, "Oh it was nothing." At that moment, in essence, what we are saying is that what God is doing through us is "nothing". Learn to recognize, acknowledge, and cooperate with the talents and abilities that God has placed in you. They are valuable. As a virtuous woman, you must get to the point where you will no longer accept discounts in any area of your life. You must value yourself as much as Jesus did because your salvation cost Him His life.

King Solomon knew that a virtuous woman was rare. The Bible tells us that he had 1,000 women in his life. Yet, he could not find one virtuous woman among all of them. He accepted a discount. What effect did these women have on Solomon, the wisest man that ever lived? They turned his heart away from God. He was surrounded by beautiful exotic women, but at the end of his life, he found himself spiritually empty and away from God. He accepted a discount because he did not listen to the advice of his mother. Solomon described the worth of a virtuous woman is far above rubies and pearls. Did you know that rubies are among the hardest gemstones and only diamonds are harder? Rubies were once called the "king of the gems." In some ancient cultures, rubies are considered the rarest and most precious gemstone in the world. In the Roman Empire, during the time of Christ, pearls were quite valuable. Julius Caesar loved pearls and was reported to have paid the equivalent of $1 million for a single pearl.

Think about how a pearl is created. It is formed when a foreign object enters the shell of an oyster. The oyster will coat the irritant with a substance called nacre. The purpose of the nacre is to cover up that irritant to protect the oyster. The mantle covers the irritant with layers of the same nacre. This nacre is used to create the shell and over a period of years, a pearl is eventually formed. Just like pearls are formed through irritants and pressure, your worth has been formed by your ability to endure and withstand hardships, difficulties, and pressure. The process of endurance and perseverance through trials has served to create a beautiful, capable, and intelligent woman who will not accept discounts for her worth.

We must learn to appreciate what God has done for us and see ourselves as valuable as He does. Many women feel unworthy of a good marriage or a good life, because of mistakes from their past or situations where they have been violated through physical, sexual, or emotional abuse. As a result, they carry shame and think they do not deserve a good life. They put up a defensive wall and refuse to open their hearts to enter into healthy relationships. Today, I want to encourage you to open yourself up to caring people around you. Don't cheat yourself or others who can benefit from your God-given talents. We need each other's gifts and abilities to serve one another. Change is painful but necessary for growth.

Change is a product of desire, association, and action. The associations you keep will greatly impact your success or failure. Which associations are you allowing to influence you? If they are a Godly influence, then follow their example. However, if your associations are not challenging you to grow in your faith or move you toward your goals, you will need to separate yourself. You cannot allow Negative Nancy to be the primary influence in your life and not expect to become like her. If you don't have a person who is mentoring you, then ask God to send you someone with more wisdom and understanding who will be willing to help guide you. When God does send you a mentor, understand that they may not be "packaged" like you think they should. They might not even be the age, race, or gender that you think they should be. The point is that if you maintain an open mind and are ready to follow their guidance, you will reach your maximum potential. However, even if you were to spend 24-hours a day, 365 days a year with any mentor but never internalize the changes they exemplify then you will not grow and develop. There comes a point in everyone's life where they must decide to change their perception in order to obtain the good, acceptable and perfect, will of God for their lives.

A woman who knows her worth will not allow others to abuse or misuse her in any way. She knows that a man who truly appreciates a precious genuine gemstone will treat her with respect and admiration. He will not mishandle that which does not belong to him. When women are pressured to give in to a situation that compromises their integrity and reputation, they are being asked for a discount. A teenage girl being pressured by a boyfriend to enter into a sexual relationship is being asked to take a discount. Unfortunately, our society has cheapened the sexual relationship to the point where women are now pursuing men. It is not uncommon for girls as young as twelve years old to be posting online and sending provocative pictures of themselves to men. Why is this? They do not know their value.

They succumb to the lie that "everyone is doing it". The idea of keeping one's virginity and purity until marriage is ridiculed in today's society and thought to be an impossible standard to uphold. What the media doesn't tell people is that sexual relationships outside of marriage carry an enormous price tag. There is no such thing as "free love". The sexual discount tears away at your soul and with each sexual encounter, a spiritual bond is made with that partner. Movies that romanticize sex outside of marriage never show the pain and humiliation that is felt when the woman finds out that she was just used as a one-night stand. The media will not tell you about the grief and guilt that is felt after an abortion.

They say that abortion is a choice that can be made because it's your body. You will try to move on with your life, but you will always remember that child. God wants to protect you from this type of pain because you are valuable. When you realize that you are virtuous, you will walk with your head held high; ready to bring about positive change in every area of your life. You will be expecting God to send you a Godly man who sees you as valuable. This man will add to you and will esteem you more than him. If you are single, don't get tired of waiting for God's best. Use this time to prepare yourself. Learn to value and protect yourself. You are not a second-rate hand me down. As you begin to see yourself through the Word of God, just like David, you will thank God, because you are fearfully and wonderfully made.

Real Worth Defined

Your worth is not defined by earthly academic accomplishments, accolades received, jobs held, family lineage, or material possessions. Your worth is not determined by a net worth spreadsheet that lists all of your material goods and then deducts the liabilities that you owe. Jesus illustrated this by asking: ***"For what is a man profited, if he shall gain the whole world, and lose his own soul? or what shall a man give in exchange for his soul?" Matthew 16:26***

No amount of earthly treasure can replace your soul. You are priceless because you are created in the image of God—plain and simple. There has never been anyone like you before, and there will never be another you. The real you is a spirit-being that is eternal; your worth is greater than anything found in this temporal world. God knows you intimately and cares for you. He feeds the birds in the air and is even aware when one of them falls from the sky. This is why Jesus instructed His disciples not to worry about what they would eat or what they would wear; because our Father knows we need these things. Jesus sums up our worth by asking them a question: *"**Are not two sparrows sold for a farthing? and one of them shall not fall on the ground without your Father. But the very hairs of your head are all numbered. Fear ye not therefore, ye are of more value than many sparrows." Matthew 10:29-31***

You are worth Jesus dying on the cross to redeem you from sin. When we are redeemed, we are deemed worthy again. Sin separates us from God, but by accepting Jesus' sacrifice, we are reconciled with God. Once you understand how precious you are to God, you will begin to value and guard yourself. You will gain strength by knowing who you are in Christ. The Proverbs 31 woman found strength in knowing that she was not like everyone else. *"**She is clothed with strength and dignity." Proverbs 31:25***

Dignity is defined as a state of being worthy, honored, or esteemed. Many times, we think of ourselves as inferior to others, because of negative situations that we've endured or painful events that occurred in our lives. These experiences can strip us of our dignity and leave us struggling with feelings of guilt, shame, insecurity, and even anger for our entire lives if we allow them to. It is not until we see ourselves through God's redemptive eyes, that we can free ourselves from these negative emotions and embrace our true identity-a new creature in Christ. *"**Therefore if any man be in Christ, he is a new creature:***

old things are passed away, behold, all things are become new." 2 Corinthians 5:17

It is our awareness of this reality that enables us to find the strength to reclaim the honor that belongs to us as God's children. He alone becomes our source of strength and dignity. Neither people's opinions of us nor their approvals will matter because our honor and self-esteem are no longer derived from others, but it is based on what God says about us. Christ strips away the old labels that people have placed on us. Today, He offers us a new start, so that we can enjoy an abundant life here on earth. The only thing we have to do is believe that He truly loves us and accept what His word says. Maybe your childhood was filled with pain, but today, you can be free from the scars of the past.

In the Old Testament Book of Esther, we encounter a young lady who unexpectedly finds herself taken from the only family she knows-a cousin named Mordecai. Esther was an orphan from birth. Her father died before she was born and her mother died during childbirth. Mordecai adopted the orphaned baby girl and raised her as his own. Esther and Mordecai were Jewish people who had been exiled from Jerusalem and held captive in the Persian kingdom. They lived in the city of Susa, which was the seat of power held by King Xerxes. Through a complex set of events, their lives became intertwined with King Xerxes.

King Xerxes' vast kingdom extended over 127 provinces and spanned from India to the Arabian Peninsula. To show off his wealth and power, Xerxes hosted a feast that lasted 180 days, for the royal princes, noblemen, and servants. In a drunken state, Xerxes sent for Queen Vashti, demanding that she enter the feast hall scantily clothed and parade herself scantily in front of these intoxicated men so that they could all see how beautiful she was. Queen Vashti refused to comply with his mandate and was banished from the kingdom for disobeying the king. She would never again be allowed to be in King Xerxes' presence.

As the days after the festival passed, the King realized what he did, and began to grieve over the loss of his beautiful wife, Vashti. When his thinking was clouded by the alcohol that he had consumed, he allowed the people on his court and wise men to counsel him on what action should be taken to address Vashti's refusal to obey his command. He had to protect his reputation, so he listened to their advice and banished her. Once he was sober, he understood the foolishness of his demand. How could he have possibly expected that his queen would parade herself in a room full of drunken men? He should have been more concerned about protecting her honor, instead of impressing the crowd. But it was too late to go back and change the past; all that remained was the aching of the lost love he carelessly tossed aside.

Everyone knew that there was no way to cancel a decree issued by the great King Xerxes. Not even he could cancel the foolish edict. As sadness filled his heart, the proud king progressively spiraled into a pit of depression and regret. His servants were concerned about his well-being and cleverly formulated a plan. His noblemen proposed a beauty contest to find a new queen. They traveled to every province to select the most beautiful virgin girls in the kingdom. These young ladies were brought to Susa to be part of the king's harem. There, they underwent twelve months of beauty treatments, which, included anointing themselves for six months with an ointment of oil and myrrh, followed by another six-month regimen of applying fragrant spices and oils. These treatments were necessary before they were presented to King Xerxes because the girl that most pleased him would be crowned the new queen.

Esther is described as a beautiful woman. I imagine she was one of those "*stop* and take another look" gorgeous women. She, unwillingly, found herself thrust into a beauty pageant that altered the course of Jewish history. Yet, despite her physical beauty, she remained humble and was not boastful or arrogant. How do we know this? As we read the book of Esther in Chapter 2, we come across one of the keys critical to her success; Esther had God's "favor" flowing in her life. Favor is defined as **fa'-ver (chen, ratson, with other Hebrew words; charis): Meaning generally goodwill, acceptance, and the benefits flowing from these...**

I believe Esther's influence came from God, because of her willingness to seek wisdom from others. Her beauty may have drawn people's eyes to her, but it was her kind heart and beautiful spirit that caused them to be willing to help her. In chapter 2, we see that her uncle Mordecai instructed her not to reveal her Jewish background to anyone, and Esther followed that advice. Then, later in that chapter when she arrives at the palace, she is placed under the care of Hegai. Hegai was the King's eunuch responsible for guarding all of these women. The Bible says that she pleased him, and she obtained kindness, another word for favor, from him. He then hand-picked seven of the palace servants to tend to her and housed them separately-in the best area of the king's harem. Did you notice how he picked out seven maids? The number seven in the Bible is often associated with perfection and completion. We are told in the book of Genesis that on the 7th day God rested from creation because all was complete. I am sure that being part of King Xerxes' harem, and becoming another one of his concubines, may not have been Esther's plan for her life. Yet, even in a harem, God's favor was moving on her behalf; quietly orchestrating and lining things up for her. The circumstances she found herself in may not have been ideal, in her way of thinking, but they were perfect in God's plan. She grew up as an orphan and now was separated from the only family she knew. Esther was forced to conceal her true identity, to survive in a palace in which she had no desire to be. Yet, through Hegai, God surrounded her with seven servants charged with protecting her.

Later, we see Esther once again seek wisdom when it was time for her to present herself before King Xerxes. All of the girls in the harem were allowed to take whatever kind of jewelry, perfume, or anything else they wanted with them when it was their turn to stand before the King. I can imagine these young women, all desiring to become the next Queen of Persia, adorned themselves with fancy clothes and extravagant jewels. Each sought to outdo the girl before her, to win King Xerxes' heart. The Bible tells us that when it was Esther's time to approach the king, she asked Hegai what he recommended she should take with her.

Notice, she had already been in the harem for at least one year, yet instead of relying on her own way of thinking, she sought advice from someone who knew more about the king than she did. Esther realized that Hegai had direct access to Xerxes and did not try to figure this out by herself. She knew that Hegai was in a position to know what the king found appealing. The Bible tells us that Esther found favor in the king's eyes, more than any other woman, and she was crowned the Queen of Persia. She was elevated from an orphan held captive in a foreign land to the first lady of the most powerful kingdom of her time.

After she was crowned Queen of Persia, Esther's life became one of privilege and ease. She had every kind of luxury at her fingertips, handmaidens were under her orders, and Esther had no concern at all. The palatial walls shielded her from the day to day sufferings of her people the Jews. As her uncle instructed, she continued to conceal her true identity. All seemed fine until the day King Xerxes' highest-ranking commander made it his mission to kill all of the Jews.

Haman was a self-centered, egotistical man who craved power and prestige. He was proud of the fact that he was an advisor to King Xerxes. One day King Xerxes issued a decree requiring all of his subjects to bow and worship his representative Haman whenever he appeared in any public setting. Haman developed animosity towards Esther's uncle Mordecai because Mordecai refused to bow down and pay homage to him. Mordecai followed Jehovah and considered it idolatry to bow down before any man. Esther received word that Mordecai was dressed in sackcloth before the palace door. Sackcloth was a coat made from coarse goat's hair and was worn when mourning the loss of a loved one or as a sign of repentance. This was a punishable offense since no one could appear before the king dressed in sackcloth.

She immediately sent one her servants to take appropriate robes down to Mordecai and find out why he was so distressed and why he was weeping and wailing throughout the city. Mordecai informed the servant that Haman had convinced King Xerxes to issue an edict commanding that every Jewish man, woman, and child throughout the entire kingdom be executed and their possessions were taken away by the executioners. He obtained permission to carry out this plan by appealing to the King's greed. Haman offered to pay 10,000 talents of silver into the King's treasury for this mass execution. This was a huge amount of money; equivalent to 750,000 pounds of silver.

To put that in perspective, at a rate of $14.00 per ounce in today's market, 10,000 talents would equate to $168 million. Mordecai sent a copy of the decree back to Esther and instructed her servant to urge her to go before the king and plead for the lives of the Jewish people. Esther read the edict and told her servant to inform Mordecai that she could not go before the king without being summoned. Everyone in the kingdom knew that it was punishable by death to appear before the king without being explicitly invited to enter into the court.

The only exception was if the king extended his golden scepter. She further explained that it had been more than 30 days since she had been called upon by the king. Mordecai rebuked her excuses and challenged her into action by causing her to reflect upon the true reason she was in the palace. He also reminded her that just because she was in the palace, it did not mean she would be spared the same fate if she remained silent. ***"Then Mordecai commanded to answer Esther, Think not with thyself that thou shalt escape in the king's house, more than all the Jews. For if thou altogether holdest thy peace at this time, then shall there enlargement and deliverance arise to the Jews from another place; but thou and thy father's house shall be destroyed: and who knoweth whether thou art come to the kingdom for such a time as this?" Esther 4:13-14***

Even in the midst of all that turmoil, Mordecai was confident that God would deliver the Jews from destruction. He saw Esther's position of influence as a channel that God could work through if she was willing to intercede on behalf of her people. However, even if Esther did not take action, Mordecai's faith caused him to believe that God's purposes would be fulfilled, and the Jews would be delivered. I believe that the phrase, "and who knoweth whether thou are come to the kingdom for such a time as this?" Burned right through every fear Esther had and, in an instant brought clarity to her very existence and purpose in life.

Inside the palace walls, Esther was temporarily shielded from the calamity that was sweeping throughout the kingdom. Her days of obscurity as a Jewish orphan girl were far behind her. She had changed her given Jewish name of Hadassah to Esther and now enjoyed a life of comfort and luxury. Within the palace, she could maintain a false sense of security if she simply kept her true identity buried deep within her. But now Esther had to question, why was she selected as Queen of Persia? Why had God shown her such favor? Esther had a monumental decision to make. Would she take a "discount" and protect her interest, or would she put her trust in Jehovah and yield her position of access and influence to achieve a greater purpose?

Without any hesitation, Esther sent her brave and wise response to Mordecai. ***"If I perish, I perish." Esther 4: 16*** She agreed to appear before the king, but only after the Jewish citizens of Shushan came together in agreement with her and her servants to unite in three days of prayer and fasting. The Jewish people of Shushan activated a spiritual principle, called the Power of Agreement, to save their nation. When we unite with other believers in prayer, Jesus stated He would be with us. ***"If two of you shall agree on earth as touching anything that they shall ask, it shall be done for them of my Father which is in heaven. For***

where two or three are gathered together in my name, there am I in the midst of them." Matthew 18:19-20

He hears our petition and will ask of the Father to answer us. The people that are coming into agreement must ask specifically of the Father and must be directly impacted by the situation. They must believe that Jesus is with them and that, by faith, they will have the things that they have asked of the Father. Faith has the courage to ask of the Father and stand in anticipation until He answers. Esther demonstrated faith, courage, and wisdom by seeking God's intervention in this matter. She did not rely on her natural charm or ability but recognized that there was power in prayer. Once again, she spent time in preparation to appear before King Xerxes.

This time, her preparation did not only consist of ointments and perfume in the natural, but it went much deeper into the spirit realm. Esther prepared her heart to hear God's strategy on how and when to petition the king. Esther and the Jewish nation came together in agreement. She sought the Lord for three days, and I believe that during that time God gave her the strategy on how to approach King Xerxes. On the third day of prayer, the Bible tells us that Esther put on her royal apparel and went into King Xerxes' courtyard.

As she confidently stood at the doorpost, the king looked up and when he saw he immediately extended his scepter towards her. Once again, because Esther sought wisdom through prayer and fasting and the scripture states that Esther found favor in the eyes of the king. Favor, we defined earlier as goodwill, acceptance, and the benefits flowing from these. Because of the favor of God flowing on her behalf, the king offered her anything she wanted, up to half of the kingdom. Esther 5:5 What was Esther's response? She simply invited the king and Haman, her people's sworn enemy, to a special dinner hosted in her palace chambers. For Esther to fully realize the potential of the position that God had prepared her for, she had to pass through the doorpost of fear and selfishness and step into a position of influence. She had to be willing to lose her life for His purpose. While Esther entertained the king and Haman, the king once again asked what she wanted. Remember, he was willing to give her up to half of his kingdom. Esther, operating under the guidance of God, simply invited both of her guests to another dinner hosted the following night. When the next evening arrived, the banquet table was set and everything was in position for Esther to plead her case. The Bible states that after the king had eaten, he asked Esther what her request was.

For Esther to obtain deliverance from her enemy, she needed God's strength to confront Haman and to expose his evil plot to the king. She began by pleading for her life and the life of her people. The king was baffled by her request. He did not know that she was a Jew until that moment when she revealed her identity. Xerxes stormed out of the banquet hall and walked through the courtyard gardens in a state of bewilderment and anger. The Bible states that Haman desperately begged Esther for mercy, and even threw himself upon her. At that moment, the king returned from the garden and saw Haman clinging to Esther. He thought that Haman was trying to sexually assault her and ordered him to be executed immediately. Haman was then executed on the very gallows he had built to hang Mordecai on. Now although Haman was no longer a threat, the original decree sentencing the Jewish people to genocide was still in place.

Esther petitioned the king to issue another decree allowing the Jewish people to defend themselves against their sworn enemies. King Xerxes agreed, and a decree was written that not only allowed the Jews to protect themselves but also granted them the right to take possession of the material goods that belonged to their slain enemies. When the people of Persia saw how God's favor had turned things around for Esther, Mordecai, and the Jewish people, the Bible says that many of them converted to Judaism. People were afraid to go against the Jews. Mordecai was placed over the house of Haman and given everything that once belonged to his sworn enemy. He was elevated to a place of leadership and authority. The Jews established the festival of Purim to serve as a reminder of how God delivered His people from destruction.

The life of Esther serves as a powerful testament to a virtuous woman who refused to accept any type of discount. She would allow neither her nationality nor the fact that she was an orphan to be used as an excuse that kept her from her destiny. She cooperated with her God-given beauty and, most importantly, sought out wisdom. Her actions demonstrated virtue to bring about change through the power of influence.

There are lessons we can learn from Esther and apply to our own lives. Like Esther, many times, we find ourselves trying to piece together the fragments left from decisions made in the wrong state of mind. We may have listened to bad advice or we were worried about what people would say about us, so we went ahead and did things without fully calculating the costs. Unfortunately, decisions made under the influence of drugs, alcohol, or stress can sometimes have long-lasting ramifications that hurt, not only ourselves but those that we love and hold closest to us.

We will find that there will be times when we cannot change the negative events of the past; however, we can always forge a new beginning. If we do not let go of the past and embrace the day that is before us, grief, anger, and regret will quickly fill our minds with worry and other negative emotions. Our minds and bodies are complex, and what you think can dramatically impact how you feel physically. It is a proven medical fact that many diseases are rooted in worry, anxiety, stress, and/or other negative emotions. These negative emotions release toxins in our bodies that, over time, can lead to numerous sicknesses including heart problems, ulcers, inflammation, and many others. Regardless of what your past has been, if you want to stay healthy and live a fulfilling life, you must find a way to accept it and move forward every day.

As we saw in the story of Esther, even when it seems like everything is spiraling out of control around us God's hand is still working on our behalf. He is there with us, even when we cannot recognize his works. Will we always find ourselves exactly where we want to be? Probably not, but it is in these moments, where if we will look closely, we too can find God's hand of provision, protection, and comfort. We can rest assured knowing that He is still working on our behalf. Favor shielded Esther from the negativity, bickering, jealousy, and everything else that was in the harem. This powerful force of favor that Esther experienced is available to us today. It can open doors of opportunity for you. How can we access favor in our lives? Let's follow Jesus' example. It is available to us by seeking and applying wisdom. ***"And Jesus increased in wisdom and stature, and in favor with God and man." Luke 2:52***

Wisdom is different than knowledge, intelligence, or I.Q. Wisdom is the ability to look at circumstances and tap into the supernatural realm to gain insight that your mind cannot easily explain where that "knowing" is coming from. Wisdom is the ability to make good decisions. For example, wisdom is the voice deep in the inside of us that some people call "intuition" or a "gut feeling." It tells you when something isn't right about a situation, even when you can't put your finger on it. That's the voice of wisdom- the Spirit of God leading and directing your steps. Jesus had wisdom that allowed Him to know people's thoughts and motives. This is why the religious leaders of His time could never trap Him with their divisive questions that were designed to set Him up. I love the fact that He never responded to the questions they asked on a surface level. Instead, His answers revealed the deceptive nature of the questions that the Pharisees and Sadducees poised. He exposed what was in their hearts. For example, when asked if people should pay their taxes or give that money to God? Jesus responded: **"Render therefore unto Caesar the things which are Caesar's; and unto God the things that are God's." Mathew 22:21**

    He would not allow himself to be trapped into political or religious debates. He used wisdom to remain true to His purpose which was drawing men into a relationship with His Father, God. This type of wisdom is available for us today if we will take time to meditate, pray, and ask God for knowledge in every area of our lives. A lack of wisdom is why we struggle with knowing how to handle our daily life. We are easily distracted from our purpose and pulled into many different paths, without knowing which direction to take.

    Many of us fail to slow down and just listen to the voice of God for our everyday concerns. We think He is not interested in things like our work, how we raise our children, the quality of our marriage, and all the other things that really matter in life. We seem to think that since these areas of our life aren't "religious or spiritual" we shouldn't involve God. In studying the book of Esther, we realize that if God cared about Esther's wellbeing while she was in King Xerxes' harem, then He also cares for every detail of our lives and is willing to guide us, if we seek wisdom. True wisdom, the ability to live life well can only be gained by tapping into the source of all life, Jesus Christ. When we invite Him to direct our decisions He can speak to us through many different methods including the wisdom and expertise of others. However, we must pursue it without limiting who God will use to speak to us.

God created us with individual talents and abilities. We can benefit in every area of our lives if we surround ourselves with people who have the expertise in the areas we do not and we tap into their insight. This does not mean that you simply look for people that you can use or have a one-sided relationship with that only benefits you. Instead, find ways to help others and when the time comes that you need insight, you will discover that people are willing to help you because you have sown seeds of kindness into the lives of others.

Godly influence is manifested when we care more about others than our own comfort. The question is whether we are willing to put aside our agenda and our interest to gain influence? Influence is a power that is greater than wealth. People will allow you to influence their lives if they see you have a genuine desire to help them. Do not discount your sphere of influence by believing the lie of the enemy trying to silence or immobilize you through fear.

All of us will face situations that will demand that we take a risk to do what is right. There are moments when we know that something is the right thing to do, even when we're not sure what the outcome will be. These times demand courageous steps of faith. The beauty is that it is during these crucial points in our lives that God reveals that He is with us as we step into our destiny. He will only reveal Himself to us to the degree that we are willing to step out of our natural thinking and step into His realm. We can access the same type of courage that Esther demonstrated by asking God to help guide us when we face difficult decisions.

Just like Esther, we often try to forget our past. We are ashamed of our mistakes or, the dysfunctional or abusive families we were born into. We are ashamed of the things people have done to hurt us. We protect ourselves by taking on a new identity and simply living within the walls of our palace. However, God sees you as more than a survivor. He is looking for people that are willing to own their moment. Are you facing a situation that demands that you carefully examine where you are today? Has God's providence placed you in a position where you can help someone? We protect ourselves by never speaking up for anyone less fortunate. We choose not to get involved in issues that demand risks and cause discomfort for us. We are afraid of what people might think about us if they knew the secrets of our past. But God says, I have brought you into my kingdom, "for such a time as this." This is the moment your past, your present, and your purpose merge and catapult you into your destiny. Someone needs to hear your story. Someone needs you to speak up for them. Someone needs you to invest in their success. You are positioned by God today, "for such a time as this".

At this point in your life, you simply cannot accept a discount. Your destiny and the destiny of those you can influence are too valuable.

Esther exemplifies the life of a virtuous woman who understood her position. She would not accept a discount by doing what was safe and easiest for her. Instead, she allowed God's plan to unfold in her circumstances and the lives of her people were saved. In chapter 3 we are going to see how Sarah, a barren woman's skeptical laughter was changed into joy by believing the impossible.

Chapter 3

Seeing Beyond Now

*"Strength and honor are her clothing;
and she shall rejoice in time to come."*
Proverbs 31:25

WHEN WAS THE LAST TIME you received news that seemed too good to be true? If you're like me, I wanted to believe what I was hearing but at the same time, I kept thinking that's just impossible. Yet, it was true. This is the scenario Abraham and Sarah faced the day Jehovah God told them she would have a son within the next year. Imagine, for a moment, that you are a seventy-five-year-old man, established in your community; having spent your working years doing what is right, and earning an honest living. Your wife is by your side and you admire her today, even more than the day you married her. As the years go by, you've seen her transformation from a pretty young lady into a stunningly beautiful woman, who has grown more attractive with every passing year. She holds your heart in her hands and you cannot imagine life without her. There is nothing you will not do for her. You know she loves you and is devoted to you, but there remains this unspoken longing in both of your hearts; the longing to have a child.

At first, you did everything to assure your wife that it was just a matter of time. You told her to relax and let nature just happen. *"If you don't obsess about it, we will have a baby,"* you found yourself telling her month after month. She questioned if the gods were mad at her or if there was something wrong with her. Eventually, she learned to accept this situation. She seems to be okay as she carries out her daily activities. Yet, every month, in the deep of night, you wake to find her weeping inconsolably. It rips at your heart because there is nothing that you can do to "fix" it. You reach out to hold her, but she lashes out-full of pain and desperation. The cycle of questioning, emptiness, anticipation, and disappointment continues. Eventually, those months turn into years of empty longing. As you look at your wife, you notice that the streaks of gray hair and the fine lines appearing on her face tell you that the dream of having your own children will never be fulfilled. It is biologically impossible. It is too late to ever hold your own child. You will never hear the cries of a baby in your home.

Then, one day, as you're somewhere lost in your thoughts and wondering if there even is a God, He speaks to you. Yes, you hear Him clearly instructing you to leave all that you know and begin to search for a land that He will guide you to. **"Now the Lord had said unto Abram, Get thee out of thy country, and from thy kindred, and from thy father's house, unto a land that I will show thee: And I will make of thee a great nation, and I will bless thee and make thy name great, and thou shalt be a blessing: And I will bless them that bless thee, and curse him who curseth thee: and in thee shall all the families of the earth be blessed." Genesis 12:1-3** At that moment, you're faced with the decision to either question if this was a supernatural encounter or step out in simple faith and obedience. *"So Abram departed, as the Lord had spoken unto him: and Lot went with him. Abram was seventy-five years old when he departed out of Haran." Genesis 12:4* This is the story of Abram and Sarai, a well-to-do couple in ancient times who worshipped the moon and other gods, until the day that Abram had an encounter with Jehovah.

God Sees It

Sometimes, in our lives, other people can see more potential in us than we can see in ourselves. They can see the painter, artist, or entrepreneurial spirit in you that you may not see. God did not see Abram as an aging man nearing the end of his life but as a man of faith. God saw Abram as a man He could work through, but ultimately, the choice was left to Abram. Would he be willing to obey? Would he actively participate and allow the blessings of God to flow through him and reach all people? Or would he remain in his comfort zone, never realizing the fullness of all that God planned for him? When God spoke to Abram, He only provided Abram with a glimpse of his redemptive plan.

Abram was not aware that God's redemptive plan required that His son Jesus would one day take the form of a human being, to stand in the place of man and bear the wage of sin for all mankind. All Abram heard was, "in you will all the families and kindred of the earth be blessed." In Abram, God was searching for a man willing to separate himself from culture, customs, and family, so that He could establish a chosen lineage through which Jesus could enter planet earth. God didn't see the limitations of Abram and Sarai's infertility. God wasn't deterred by the fact that

Abram and Sarai had no children. Those things were irrelevant to God when He said, "I will make of you a great nation." God saw in Abram a man that He could use to reach the world if Abram was willing to obey. God simply issued a command and left Abram with a decision. Webster's Dictionary defines a nation as: ***A people having a common origin, tradition, and language and capable of forming or actually constituting a nation-state b: an ethnic group constituting one element of a larger unit (as a nation).***

How do you make a nation out of two senior citizens well past their child-bearing years? If you looked at the natural, you would never imagine that Abram and Sarai would be the patriarch and matriarch of a great nation. God saw a man who would fear, would lie, and would fail in his own abilities. Yet, God also saw in Abram a man who would be willing to obey and take immediate action. A man who would leave his home and everything he knew out of sheer obedience and total surrender to a God he didn't know. God saw a couple that was willing to obey. He saw that they would fear, lie, and take matters into their own hands. Yet, He also saw a man that would love Him above everything and everyone.

Abram knew that he had heard from God and he took action. Many times, when we hear from God, we don't take immediate action. We question if we're really "hearing from God" or if it's just wishful thinking. But, when we delay our obedience, we leave the door open for the enemy to plant seeds of doubt and uncertainty. One way of determining if something is from God is to search it out in scripture. Anything God is telling you to do will not be contrary to His written Word found in the Bible. If Abram would have postponed his departure from Ur, then I am sure many of his neighbors would have talked him out of leaving. They would have expressed their concern about the travel conditions. They would have questioned the wisdom of leaving behind wealth, comfort, and security. They would have ridiculed him for believing that he would have a son. He would have experienced all of the same things society questions us about when we are stepping out in faith and doing what God is challenging us to do.

There are pivotal moments in each of our lives when we will be challenged to leave our comfort zone and follow God. We won't have everything figured out, but there will be an inward "knowing," deep within us, that to gain something greater, we must venture out. Each one of us will face our departure. For some, it may be leaving the church that their family has been part of for years. For others, it might be starting a new career, or making a geographical move. Regardless of the circumstance, each one of these scenarios requires us to leave what we've known, to obtain what we "see" in our spirits. Through the eyes of faith, we "see" things being better, although, we're not sure how it will happen. Most of the time, we don't have all of the pieces fitting nicely together. We just have to step out in faith, with only the assurance that God is with us.

The process may be quick, or it may be a sequence of events. It's only after you step back and reflect that you can see the progression God orchestrated. Years ago, my husband George and I began our journey out of our Ur. We were living in a small town in Ohio. We both grew up there and had friends, family, and many connections to the community. We knew that God had called us into some type of ministry, but we weren't exactly clear where or what it would be. We were very active in our church, serving as Associate Pastors, responsible for leading the music ministry and I also taught adult Bible classes. We didn't know it at the time but 1996 was going to be the beginning of many changes for us. Up until that point in our marriage, we had never experienced any type of financial difficulty. George was working for a company in the natural gas industry and I was a Marketing Manager within the telecommunication industry. It was my first job out of college, so I thrust myself whole-heartedly into my career. Then, after six years, there came the news of a pending company merger. People within the company were panicked, knowing their jobs would likely be eliminated. They had devoted years of their lives building the company. They could not grasp the fact that all they had worked hard to achieve was coming to an end. Many were angry and felt betrayed by the company's owners. They had envisioned retiring from the company and enjoying a secure pension. Now they faced an unknown future.

During those months of transition, it seemed like everything was suspended and hanging by a thread. Contractual obligations kept me from leaving the company until after the merger. While trying to assure the employees that things were going to work out with the new company, I was also clinging to the hope that maybe somehow, my job would be spared. I too felt their fears and uncertainty. There were months of suspension-almost as if my life was like a slice of lemon inside of a glass of water just floating with no real movement and surrounded by many uncertainties. There was nothing I could do to change it. All I could do was wait to see if a manager in another part of the country, who didn't know me, would deem my position valuable to their new organization. The industry awards I'd won, the nights I'd spent away from my home traveling, and all the extra hours I'd worked would not matter anymore. It would come down to a simple business decision.

Then, the day arrived that the merger was finalized. The anticipation was finally over, and my position was eliminated. There was finally closure and now I had to move forward with the "facts." At first, the change was surreal. I just felt as though I was on an extended vacation. But, after the fourth week without a job, I remember the sense of loss that swept over me. It was a Sunday evening and, as I got ready for bed, I began to weep uncontrollably. I realized that, for the first time in my adult life, I didn't have anywhere to be on Monday morning. I became depressed and began to question my self-worth. It was difficult to explain but somehow, I had allowed my job to define "who" I was. Up until that point, I worked so hard to get my degree, so I could get a good job and be seen as a "somebody" by others. My self-esteem came from the boards I served on, the people with whom I was connected with and the community functions in which I was invited to participate. I allowed my work to become my identity and devoted myself completely to my job. Then, in a moment it was all gone, and I was no longer needed.

God used this event to show me how I had put my career before Him, by trusting in a company to be my financial source. God promises to be our provider. The Bible states that God is a loving Father and He is concerned about the everyday affairs of our lives. I believe God allowed this transition to occur so that I could begin to separate from my natural understanding and ways of doing things. God wanted me to totally trust Him for the daily bread that I needed. I had to place my career in His hands and know that my worth is not defined by a paycheck, job title, or what others say about me. My worth is determined by the fact that God loves me. He sees me as valuable.

I realized that I would find the most personal satisfaction by fulfilling what God created me to do on this earth. What I mean, is that God is our Creator. He created us for a specific purpose in life. If I choose to focus my energy, time, and resources fulfilling my agenda, and never give thought to what I was placed on this earth to do, chances are, I will not fulfill my destiny and will feel frustrated. If I spend my life trying to please people and do not develop my God-given abilities, then I am cheating mankind and myself. When I "lost" my job, I gained insight. I was given an opportunity to pause and reflect on the direction my life was taking. God was calling me to leave the land of Ur because He had something greater in store. Ur represents our security, our way of doing things, our associations, and even the source of our identity.

At some point in their lives, every human being must answer this fundamental question: why was I created and what must I accomplish here on this earth? God wants to lead us into our destiny if we are willing to lean on Him completely. He will lead us in stages, as we learn to hear His voice and trust His character. The three years after I lost my job continued to be a period of change and increased dependence on God. Our daughter, Adina, was born in 1998 and I was a stay-at-home mother. We were doing fine, financially, and were adjusting to our new family. Then, it happened again. The company George was working for announced that they had been purchased. In a matter of months, his position was eliminated, and we were faced with the question of what are going to do now? It wasn't a time of panic for us, but rather a time of expectation. We knew that God was going to lead us into something new and we were waiting for His direction.

My heart was set on moving to Texas to be closer to my parents and extended family. George was not sure and wisely suggested that we take our time and not make any hasty decisions. During this period of waiting, he was able to serve as part of a missionary team that provided leadership training to the Pastors in the remote mountains of Guatemala. While he was there, he witnessed God's miraculous healing power and saw God bring a little girl back to life. In Guatemala, he connected with a Pastor and his wife, who were preparing to serve as missionaries to the Muslims in the Middle East. These were life-changing events that George would never have experienced if we were anxious about our finances and the fact that we didn't have a "plan" in place. All we knew was that if God allowed our material circumstances to change, then He would provide for us.

After George's return from Guatemala, he was determined to obtain more training and preparation for full-time ministry. We looked at various Bible schools and some generous friends offered to help us relocate closer to them so that we could enroll in their church's school. Even though it seemed like a good opportunity, and we had family in these areas, there wasn't a release in our hearts to move in that direction. There just seemed to be something holding us back. We prayed and waited.

Then, through a friend, we were introduced to Dr. Joseph Rodriguez. Dr. Rodriguez is a gifted anointed Pastor and Bible school teacher. Our friend invited him to speak at a conference he was hosting, and George attended one of the meetings. When George came home, I could see there was something different about him. He was excited and could hardly wait to go back to the next meeting. Later that week, George and I listened to a tape series that he was given by Dr. Rodriguez. In one of the audiotapes, Dr. Rodriguez mentioned that he taught at the Bible school he had founded. We instantly knew that we needed to go and visit the school. We made arrangements to attend a Sunday morning service and, from the minute we walked in, we sensed that this was where God was leading us.

During our three-hour trip home, we meditated on the message the Pastor taught and kept talking about how we deeply sensed the presence of God in such a tangible way. I remember saying to George how much I would love to sit under that type of teaching ministry, if only it wasn't so far away. We decided to attend one of the Bible School Open House sessions that was slated for early that spring. I'll never forget sitting in that class and being taught the basic principles of walking by faith. It was as if blinders were being removed from my eyes, as I saw through the scriptures for the first time, how it is impossible to please God without faith.

Yes, I had received my salvation through faith in Jesus Christ, but that was all I had applied my faith to. For years I read about how Christ has given us power over the devil, the enemy of our soul, but I never really understood how to apply my faith to use that authority to obtain success in every area of my life. After the classes were over, we headed back to Ohio and we both knew that this is where God was calling us. We had to obey and go, even though we didn't know anyone there. We didn't have family there. We didn't have jobs lined up. All we had was faith that, if we moved in obedience, God would provide for us.

We knew that to obtain what God had for us, we would need to be taught and mentored. This process would require us to leave our way of doing things, our familiar surroundings, and our security nest and venture into a new location, church, and community. We announced our plans in May and by Labor Day we moved to Michigan and enrolled in Bible School. Looking back at it now, that move was one of the greatest leaps of faith we have ever taken. It was difficult and lonely. There were times when we struggled financially because we didn't find jobs as soon as we moved to Michigan, but God provided for us. Leaving our "Ur" brought us closer together as a family and it deepened our dependence on God and each other. As we went through the first year of Bible School, there were many occasions when we questioned if we had heard from God. We questioned if we had made a mistake and we thought about returning to Ohio. George and I both encouraged each other; we clung to the promise in God's word that He would not leave us. We were determined to graduate from Bible School together. The past was "safe," but we knew it would be a great tragedy to return to the safety of our "Ur" and miss what God had destined for us to complete.

There are so many people trapped with a burning desire to venture out into their dream, but they are bound by fear. Fear of losing property. Fear of what people will say about them if they venture into something new. Don't allow material possessions, people, or circumstances keep you from obeying the prompting of God gently nudging you into the direction you should go. Remember the rich young ruler who came to Jesus and asked what he needed to do inherit eternal life? Jesus responded: ***"If though will be perfect, go and sell that thou hast, and give to the poor, and thou shall have treasure in heaven; and come and follow me." Matthew 19:21***

The Bible says the young man turned away, saddened because he had much material wealth. Was Jesus teaching that being materially wealthy is wrong? No. Jesus knew that this young man loved money even though he was very religious by all outward appearances, the love of money kept him from experiencing the joy of being one of Jesus' disciples. The cost was too high, and he was unwilling to leave his "Ur".

When God calls us to grow closer to Him, it can be frightening at first, but it can also be the most exciting journey you can imagine, and it all starts with one simple step of faith. When God called Abram, God saw a man who would be willing to leave all to obtain his destiny. What about you? What are you willing to leave to obtain God's best?

Hysterical Faith

Ten years would come and go between the time God spoke his promise to Abram and Sarai and there was still no baby. Sarai questioned if it was her "fault," as she began to experience the onset of menopause. She felt helpless because she could not turn back the hands of time. Then one day, Sarai glimpsed over at her servant Hagar. As Sarai noticed Hagar's vitality and youthfulness, she instantly formulated a plan. Yes, there was a way that she and Abram could have a son. It's simple, she reasoned, all she had to do was persuade Abram to take Hagar as a surrogate mother. They decided to take matters into their own hands to have this promised child. She rationalized that ten long years had passed since God promised them a child. Maybe He had changed His mind. Sure, having a surrogate child was not the way she expected things to work out, but at least Abram would finally have a son; an heir. Sarai convinced herself that she would love the child as her own because she was within her legal rights to take the child borne from her servant. However, after Hagar conceived, things quickly became a nightmare as contempt rooted itself in Sarai's heart.

What is amazing to me is that none of Sarai's plotting and convincing Abram to participate in her plot surprised

God. He knew they would take this course of action and He did nothing to stop it. Abram could have refused to be involved in Sarai's scheme. God could have intervened and sent an angel to warn him not to go through with the plan. But God didn't do anything to stop them. Why? Because, just like us, Abram and Sarai were created, in the image of God, with a free-will. God knew their faith would fail, but when He appeared to them, 13 years later, He called them by their new names, which represented what He saw in them.

He called Abraham, the Father of Many Nations, and Sarah, Princess when there was still no baby. He saw past all of their faults and, almost twenty years later, still continued to call them according to His perfect plan. God foresaw the tension that would be in Abraham's household, because of Ishmael; the baby born by Hagar. He knew there would be animosity between Sarah and Hagar and that, eventually, Abraham would feel the pain of forcing the boy and his mother out of his household. Abraham would be torn between the love he felt for Ishmael and the woman he loved. God foreknew the bitter consequences that Abraham and Sarah would suffer because they chose to take matters into their own hands; instead of waiting for His perfect timing. But still, He called them according to their destiny. The God-kind of faith sees beyond our failures and the consequences of those choices.

Maybe you've failed God and you feel condemned. In the moment you knew that the decision you were about to make was wrong, but you went along with it because you had grown impatient. It wasn't the best thing for your life, but you were willing to accept it. Now, you're faced with the consequences of that decision and you don't think you can ever pick up your walk with God again. Let me assure you this is not the case. Don't be discouraged. God is still calling you by your purpose and waiting for you. God has faith in you and His faith sees past your failure. The God-kind of faith is what is urging you, right now, to get back on track and pursue your dream with renewed zeal. It may not seem easy to do, because you feel that you're too far off course, but God, through the voice of faith, is prompting you to start over again.

At the age of ninety-nine, God appears to Abram, again, and tells him that Sarai will have a child within a year. What happens next is an example for us to follow. **"Then Abraham fell upon his face and laughed and said in his heart, Shall a child be born unto him that is an hundred years old? And shall Sarah, that is ninety years old bear a son?" Genesis 17:17** We see Abraham fall on his face, as a sign of worship and begin to laugh. This was the kind of laughter that was one filled with faith, grasping a hold of what God promised and "seeing" it as a done deal. Look closely at Abraham's reaction. He was ecstatic! He was rolling on the floor laughing and rejoicing because God's timing had finally come into fruition. His question was more of a statement of how miraculous this news was. This baby was going to be born, even though he was 100 and Sarah was 90. What we need to learn from Abraham is that *faith laughs!* He didn't wait until Sarah got past her first trimester, making sure everything was going to be okay before he started rejoicing. Abraham didn't have to see Sarah's belly begin to show before he believed. No. God spoke it and Abraham considered it as good as done. Abraham learned that God is a God of His Word.

How Can That Be?

God appeared to Abraham on a second occasion. This time the Word of the Lord was intended to be heard by

Sarah. Abraham was sitting outside his tent when three visitors arrived. He immediately discerned that it was the Lord and he instructed his servants to prepare a meal for the weary travelers. As they were preparing the meal, the Angel of the Lord asked for Sarah. Abraham responds that she was helping to prepare the meal. Remember, women were not allowed to interact with foreigners or men in that time and culture. But our mighty God knew exactly where Sarah was located. He knew she was just on the other side of the tent wall within an earshot and was listening to every word. The Lord began to repeat the prophecy to Abraham reminding him that Sarah would have a son by this time next season. We read that Sarah laughed and questioned: *"Shall I of a surety bear a child, which am old?" Genesis 18:13* The Lord immediately confronted her unbelief and questioned why she said: *"Shall I of a surety bear a child, which am old? Is anything too hard for the Lord? At the time appointed I will return unto thee, according to the time of life, and Sarah shall have a son." Genesis 18:13-14.*

As we read on, we find that, out of fear, Sarah tried to deny the fact that she laughed, but God, once again, would not be deceived and confronted her with the truth. She did laugh, but it was different than Abraham's laughter. Her laugh stemmed from doubt and unbelief. Why did she doubt? She continued to look at the natural. All she could see was barrenness. As she looked at her body, over the years, she lost hope and accepted the fact that it was biologically impossible for them to conceive. But I believe that God dealt with her unbelief head-on so that she would renounce doubt and get the focus off of her body and onto God's promise. The Bible tells us in Hebrews 11:11: *"Through faith also Sarah herself received strength to conceive seed, and was delivered of child when she was*

past age, because she judged him faithful who had promised."

Like Sarah, it is time for believers to begin trusting the hand of the Lord again. While we doubt, God is patiently asking "Is there anything too hard or too wonderful for Me to do?" He's waiting for us to believe that He can and wants to do what seems impossible in the natural. When was the last time you dared to dream and ask God for the impossible? Maybe the "impossible" for you is a happy marriage. You've been disappointed by previous relationships, so the thought of a truly fulfilling marriage is something you think you cannot have. He's asking you today, *"Is there anything too hard for Me? Is there a home that's too hard for me to provide? Is it impossible for Me to give you a child? Is it impossible for Me to open doors for you to have a fulfilling career? Is it impossible for Me to send you around the world as a missionary, evangelist, or teacher?"* When we focus on His abilities and not our limitations, we begin to understand the words of Jesus: **"With men this is impossible, but with God all things are possible." Matthew 19:26**

We must learn that, even though His timing may be different than ours, His timing is perfect. Just like Abraham and Sarah, we must stand in faith, to receive the fulfillment of our dreams and desires. God is eternal. He does not operate on our 24-hour day system. He does not measure time the way we humans do in days, weeks, months, and years. He operates in the realm of faith, which is the realm of Now. What do I mean by the Now realm? Since God is a spirit, He has no start or finish. He saw Abraham and Sarah holding baby Isaac, before the foundation of the earth when nothing was created. God saw you before you were born, and He gave you your name. Jeremiah 1:5 He sees the end before it happens' which, is why He doesn't see us as defeated, beat down, or destroyed. He sees us as victorious, through His Son, Jesus Christ. He sees us in Christ. Yesterday, today, and tomorrow are all the same to Him.

Oftentimes, God speaks to us through other people. They might come up and tell you how much they enjoyed something you did. Through their compliments, your gifts are being recognized. Learn to give the Lord the honor and glory for gifting you and graciously accept the compliment. When they ask you when you are going to venture into something new, don't laugh in disbelief. Look at the scripture. God called Sarah out for laughing in disbelief, as she overheard what was being prophesied. God rebuked her, at that moment, so that she would change her disbelief and come into agreement with His Word, thus releasing His supernatural power in her body, so that she could conceive.

We may have a natural inclination toward certain activities, but we don't acknowledge or cooperate with the ability lying dormant within us. Many of you have gifts lying dormant. The only person laughing and holding you back through doubt is you. You hear the jeers in your mind saying things like, *"Yeah, right, you'll never own your beauty salon, you'll never record that CD. The ministry you've always dreamed of will never be launched because nobody knows you."* All of these negative thoughts overwhelm your thinking, and you forget the fact that this year, there is going to be a New Artist of the Year, who is going to sell millions of recordings. In every town in America, there is a busy beauty salon. You have to realize that there is a place in the market for your unique talents and abilities.

Today is the right time for you to look at the future and laugh. Rejoice over the revelation of what your life can be. Faith gets hysterical. It sees beyond the now. As you laugh in expectation, you are releasing faith, which is power. Just like Sarah, you must deal with unbelief head-on, so that virtue can strengthen you to conceive and give birth to your desires. You cannot obtain all that God has for your life if you are unwilling to let go of the past. In chapter 4 we are going to examine the danger of idleness and the true cost of just going along with the status quo.

Chapter 4

Losing the Rearview Mirror

"She looketh well to the ways of her household,
and eateth not the bread of idleness."
Proverbs 31:23

THINK ABOUT WHAT it would be like to see a "motion picture" in your mind of something that happened to you ten, twenty, or even thirty years ago. You are the star in this "motion picture" vividly recalling what you had for breakfast, what you wore that day and even the significant world events that you read about or heard on the news. You remember exactly how you felt that day, who you talked with, what you ate, and even what day of the week a certain date fell on. Imagine if, at any moment, something in the present could trigger a memory from your past that would then spark another memory of a different day. It would be a never-ending cycle of past memories. This is a real scenario for some people. This condition has recently been diagnosed as hyperthymesia-the inability to forget. It is a condition in which an individual possesses a superior autobiographical memory, meaning he or she can recall the vast majority of personal experiences and events in his or her life. Would you find that ability a blessing or a burden? Jill Price, one of the first persons to be diagnosed with Hyperthtymesia,[1] describes her condition as a "burden,"[2] because she is constantly getting lost in the past. It is hard for her to take care of today or plan for the future because her mind is permanently living in the past.

In the same manner, many people are emotionally idle. They are held captive and tied to events, disappointments, or losses from their past. They painfully try to move forward with their lives, but, day after day, they vividly remember an event or multiple events and become emotionally frozen in the past. As difficult as it may seem, there is hope for you. This hope does not come from positive thinking or constant self-affirmation, but from the healing words spoken by Jesus. His words can wash the pain and regrets of the past. His words can heal your broken and wounded heart and enable you to lose the rearview mirror once and for all. ***"The Spirit of the Sovereign LORD is on me, because the LORD has anointed me to preach good news to the poor. He has sent me to bind up the brokenhearted, to proclaim freedom for the captives and release from darkness for the prisoners." Isaiah 61:1***

When Jesus walked the face of the earth, He stated that God sent Him to bind up the brokenhearted. In my research for this book, I discovered that when bones break, the supply of blood that keeps the bone healthy is cut off. Therefore, it is important to immediately set that bone back to its original place, so that the blood supply can return, and the cells and tissue can begin to knit the fractured ends back together. This healing doesn't happen immediately. For healing to occur, the injured bone must be reset and bound. In the same way, if you have been injured emotionally, you must identify the source of your pain and deal with it directly. How do you deal with it directly? You must acknowledge that what has happened to you was wrong and painful. If you were a victim of violence or abuse, then the situation was not your fault and you did nothing to deserve being mistreated because you are a child of God created in His image. What happened to you was designed by the enemy, Satan, to destroy your life. But God is with you and now you can experience restoration. Just as if you had a broken bone, you must allow God's spirit to give you the strength to immobilize the painful memory and leave it in the past.

Now imagine a person who had a broken arm and, after wearing the cast for two months, is told by the doctor that the x-rays show the bone is completely healed. He sees the doctor's assistant coming into the room to remove the cast and then, he abruptly refuses to allow them to remove it. The patient is afraid that the assistant is going to hurt him again, by removing the cast, and he's heard that therapy is painful, so he has decided that he doesn't want to go through it. He tells the assistant that he's okay just the way he is. He's become used to the cast and has even adapted to the limitations of his arm. You would think this was very foolish because he was allowing his fear to keep him bound to a past injury. In the same way, many people are afraid to move forward, because of the unknown. They have adapted to their own "emotional cast" to keep themselves from engaging in new relationships, new opportunities, and new ways of thinking or believing. They have chosen to go through life with limited mobility because they refuse to walk in the freedom that is theirs through Christ Jesus. They do this all in a vain effort to protect themselves from hurt and pain. Instead of looking forward to a life that is fully restored, they eat the bread of idleness. They do this by speaking about the past and they keep looking back.

Jesus' love has come to cast out darkness in every area of our hearts and minds. You must exercise your spiritual muscle and begin to study the scriptures about who you are in Christ Jesus today. Your life today is not defined by one bad decision, one failed marriage, one abortion, or your past drug addiction. Your life today is defined by whether you are alive in Christ Jesus. You can enter into His life by accepting Him as Messiah, healer of the brokenhearted. As you walk in this new life, you will be able to exercise your spiritual muscles and leave the past alone.

Lot's Wife Looks Back and Loses Her Destiny

In the book of Genesis, we find a nameless woman, who is only identified as, "Lot's wife." Lot was the nephew of the Jewish Patriarch, Abraham. The Bible tells us that Lot was blessed by God, because of his association with Abraham. God's blessing upon them caused their flocks of sheep and cattle to multiply and increase so much so that Lot's shepherds were constantly fighting with Abraham's shepherds because the green pastures could not sustain both flocks. Eventually, to maintain peace between their servants, Abraham and Lot agreed to separate.

As an unselfish and caring uncle, Abraham took Lot to a high mountain and granted him the first choice of the area in which he wanted to live. Abraham agreed to accept whatever land Lot did not want. As Lot looked out, he saw that the topography of Sodom and Gomorrah was lush and very green, so he selected that land. He was lured by the rolling hills and abundance of water and green fields. The only problem with Sodom and Gomorrah was that the Bible described it as extremely wicked.

As the story continues, we aren't told how long Lot and his family lived in this city, but we do know that he and his wife built a home along the city wall. The Bible states that God determined that He was going to destroy the cities, because of the sexual sins that existed. Before the destruction of the cities, God sent two angels to lead Lot and his family into safety and freedom. When the angels arrived at Sodom and Gomorrah, dusk was quickly turning into night. Lot saw the visitors arrive and hastily arose from where he was seated along the city's gate and, to protect them from being attacked, invited the men into his home. Lot did not yet realize that these men were angels.

As they arrived at Lot's home, I imagine they are met by his wife; a woman who had grown accustomed to a lifestyle of opulence and luxury. She knew that the activities of the city were displeasing to God, but she easily ignored them, because she foolishly thought they didn't directly affect her. She deceived herself into thinking that she is protected from the sin all around her, by remaining inside the walls of her home. She had grown idle. Her primary concern was the comfort of her family and enjoying the finest things that money could buy. When she went into the city, the actions that were once shocking and appalling no longer caused her to turn her head and look away. She determined not to offend members of her community by speaking up against the dangers of living contrary to God's commandment. After living in Sodom for so many years, her daughters had married men from the community.

Lot's family was now firmly rooted in Sodom's high society. Her life was carefree, and she enjoyed the finest of everything, until the day these strange men arrived. She heard the uproar building outside of her home, as the crowd demanded that Lot send the visitors out to them. Almost instantly the crowd was incited into an angry riotous mob; beating down her home demanding that Lot send these two men out. Lot and his family had never seen the city in so much chaos and, out of sheer desperation, Lot stepped outside of his home and tried to pacify the crowd because he realized these visitors were not mere men, but they were angels sent by God. The crowd was so consumed by lust for the visitors, that they refused his daughters and threatened to treat him even worse than the visitors if he did not turn them over. A mob-mentality spread like wild-fire amongst them and they continued to siege Lot's home.

Finally, the angels stepped outside to save Lot and demonstrated their power by temporarily blinding the entire crowd, while they pulled Lot into his home. The angels instructed Lot to find his daughters and sons-in-law and get out of the city before sunrise because they were going to destroy it. Lot's wife was bewildered and confused by how quickly her world was collapsing around her. Shielded by the darkness of night, Lot went to the homes of his sons-in-law and told them they had to flee the city to escape its coming destruction, but instead of listening to the warnings, they made fun of him and thought that he is joking. What happened? How did Lot lose his leadership position within his own family? Maybe they did not respect Lot, because instead of instructing them in the ways of God, he participated in their carefree living? Or worse yet, although he saw that their lifestyle was displeasing to God, he did not want to offend them, so he simply sat by and watched them, and did not instruct them until this night- when it was too late.

For so many years, Lot and his wife lived passively in their city, knowing that evil was all around them, and said nothing. They ate the bread of idleness spiritually speaking. They did not warn their families; they did not stand up for righteousness; and although they might not have participated in the sin, their passivity was about to cost them everything. Lot's passivity caused him to lose his place of moral leadership within his family. This should be a lesson for every parent. We must never relinquish or ignore our position as spiritual leaders to our children. It does not matter how old they are or what lifestyle they choose to live. As parents, we will stand before God and give an account as to whether or not we instructed them to live Godly lives.

Yes, God has created every person with their free-will, but numerous times throughout the bible, He has commanded parents to instruct their children. It is very sad to live in our society where so many parents are consumed with seeking material gain. They foolishly think that the things and possessions they buy their children will compensate for time not spent with them. We hear the pain in the voices of so many young people who come from broken marriages where each parent seeks to live their own life, without truly considering what is best for their children. Parents should not give society the responsibility of raising their children. We cannot rely on the school system, youth groups, after-school programs, or even the church to give the only instruction they receive on how to live a moral life. What society calls good may be contrary to what the Bible calls good. It is up to you to live your life in such a way that demonstrates to your children what is pleasing to God in a real way. If you do not accept your position as, not only a provider for their physical needs, but also as their spiritual leader, the day will come when you look back and see your child going down a destructive path. Instead of listening to you, just like Lot's sons-in-law, they will just laugh and think you're joking, because they have lost all respect for you.

I can imagine the bewilderment that Lot and his family must have felt. In a daze, he slowly started to gather a few belongings together, not sensing the urgency of the looming destruction, until the angels forcefully grabbed him, his wife, and two daughters by the hand and physically escorted them out of the city. As the angels hurriedly lead them, they commanded Lot's family to run to the mountain. They were told not to look back or stop along the way or they would be destroyed. Nevertheless, Lot replied and says to the angels that the mountain was too far away and that he could not make it that far. He requested permission to escape to a small village, named Zoar, that was nearby, and the angels granted his request. Zoar seemed like a good place to Lot, away from Sodom, but not too far away. God was directing him to start a new life in the mountains, but Lot wanted to settle in the comfort of a tiny place, Zoar.

Oftentimes, we too want God to intervene and protect us from our problems. He wants to give us a new start, but we think we can do it our way. He wants to place us on the mountaintop that He knows will offer tremendous opportunity, but all we see are our limitations. We are weary and don't think we can climb another mountain just to start all over again. So, we ask if we can just stay in Zoar; a comfortable tiny place. We limit our new start, based upon the weariness we feel. The current struggles have taken our energy and we back down from "fighting another uphill battle." We will all face mountains of obstacles and opportunities in our lives. However, it is when we climb to the mountain top that we gain perspective on what's on the other side. On the mountain top, we can look back and see how far we've come, but what is even more important, is that we can see what's in front of us.

We can see God's plans and His purposes if we're willing to take one step at a time and lean on Him to lift us. He's our safety harness, foothold, and sustainer. He wants to bring us into new lands of rest and restoration if we will simply trust Him. As Lot and his family reached their safe haven, they looked up and saw the clouds thicken and they heard thunderous lightning. They remembered the warnings of the angels and firmly fixed their eyes straight ahead. They knew they could not look back; they must not stop.

Finally, Lot's wife could no longer continue. They were on the verge of salvation and she could hear the destruction behind her, but her heart was tied to Sodom. She could not restrain herself from looking back to catch one more glimpse of her treasured city. As she heard the sounds of calamity, she turned back to see the destruction. Perhaps she was frightened of starting all over again and she desired just one more glimpse of her beautiful house and treasures. She relied on her wealth and material possessions, instead of depending on God. She had forgotten that it was God who had blessed them and allowed them to prosper and succeed. If He was merciful to deliver them, then He would certainly allow them to rebuild their lives. She looked back for a glimpse of what she thought was "security". She could not believe that there was something better waiting ahead of them. The pain of losing her possessions pulled at her heart and when she thought of it all being destroyed, she turned back. ***"For where your treasure is, there will your heart be also." Luke 12:34***

If we truly want to enjoy the fullness of God's plan in our lives, we need to carefully guard our hearts, because what we esteem the most will drive the decisions we make. She valued material things and her possessions over the Word of God. God gave them explicit instructions not to turn back, but because her possessions had preeminence in her heart, she disobeyed God and looked back, only to see the rubbish of the city, and she became a pillar of salt. Many people are holding on to relationships, memories or events from the past that hold them as a prisoner. These things in our past can be both good and bad. However, God is a God of Now. He is active in our lives today and has plans for our future. Maybe you've experienced a tragedy in your past and are haunted by the nightmares that make the event seem like it just happened yesterday. God can set you free. God is with you now. ***"Remember ye not the former things, neither consider the things of old. Behold, I will do a new thing: now it shall spring forth, shall ye not know it? I will even make a way in the wilderness, and rivers in the desert." Isaiah 43:18-19***

God was going to do a new thing with Lot and his family. However, for them to start over, they could not dwell in the past. God wants you to see that He can do a new thing in your life, but for us to obtain it, you've got to do the three things found in Isaiah:

1) Forget the former things
2) Don't dwell on the past
3) See a new thing

Forgetting the former things requires effort on our part. God is not going to suddenly remove every painful memory, but He has given us the ability to choose to forget them. Webster's dictionary defines forgetting as: ***a: to lose the remembrance of: be unable to think of or recall; to cease from doing; to treat with inattention or disregard; to cease remembering or noticing.***

Do you see that last definition...? To cease remembering or noticing; to treat with inattention or disregard. We need to renew our thinking and focus our attention on positive ideas, gaining a deeper understanding of God's Word, and applying biblical principals in our life. When we preoccupy ourselves with these things, we don't have time to keep digging up the mess from our past. We don't deny the bad things that have happened in our past, but by forgetting them, we release ourselves from the dead-weight that keeps us stagnant and unhappy in life.

The second principle we see here is that God does not want us to dwell in the past. God is a God of Now. He doesn't have a timeframe and is not confined by time, as we know it. Therefore, anytime we are dealing with things in the spirit realm, we are dealing with timeless truths. As human beings, we are created as a three-part being. We have a physical body, which, is in contact with this earth and is governed by the five senses. This outer part is the part that others can see, but it is not eternal. The body becomes sick, tired, and ages. We also have a soul. The soul is the part of you that governs your thinking, your emotions, and your will. The last part of you is your spirit. It is the eternal part of you. It is the real you that will either live forever in heaven with God or will be eternally separated from Him. God communicates with your spirit. This is why people will go to church and can't explain why they feel like crying or they feel peaceful. It is because their spirit is receiving power from God, as His word is being taught.

God gives us a gift every day. This gift is the ability to determine where we will allow our mind/soul to dwell. Will we remain idle every day with the same old problems? Or, will we embrace each day as the greatest day of our lives? I remember the first time our Pastor, Dr. Rodriguez stated this. "This is the greatest day of your life. Yesterday is over and you can't do anything about it. You can't change it; you can't relive it. Tomorrow is not here so today is the greatest day of your life." God is saying the same thing. If you want to create the best life possible, then you must choose to live in the now. You cannot dwell in the past. To dwell means: **to remain for a time; to live as a resident; to keep the attention directed; to speak or write insistently.**

Where are you living today? Are you living in the now of God or are you living as a permanent resident in Shameville? Do you find yourself constantly talking to anyone who will listen about how someone offended you or how someone did you wrong? Are you still trying to figure out what you could have done differently that might have changed the outcomes of the past? The Apostle Paul clearly understood the danger of living in the past when, under the inspiration of the Holy Spirit, wrote to the Philippians: **"Brethren, I count not myself to have apprehended; but this one thing I do, forgetting those things which are behind, and reaching forth unto those things which are before, I press toward the mark for the prize of the high calling of God in Christ Jesus." Philippians 3:13-14**

During his ministry, he had seen thousands of people come to the saving knowledge of Jesus Christ. He wrote most of the New Testament and established thriving churches throughout the Roman Empire and Asia Minor. These were things that most ministers would consider great accomplishments, but he declared, *"I forget what is behind me and strain toward what is ahead. I press toward the goal for the prize of the upward call of God in Christ Jesus."* He refused to stay locked to the past and was willing to push toward the high calling. Each one of us also has the upward call of God upon our lives. Your goal may be different than mine, but the point is that we must all press forward and upward. Forgetting is a choice. Today, you can lose the rear-view mirror that keeps you stagnant. You can press forward and strain to what is ahead in your life. When I read scripture, I imagine a very competitive relay race, where the baton is carefully transferred from one runner to the other. The runner receiving the baton takes a quick glance back to see his fellow teammate coming along, but to win the race; he must keep his eyes focused on the finish line. The baton is handed off to him and he strains forward with every ounce of strength and energy he can muster. We are all running this race of life. We must press forward and keep our eyes firmly fixed on the prize, which, is in Christ Jesus.

A virtuous woman looks well to the ways of her household. She doesn't eat the bread of idleness. To be idle means to spend time doing nothing or to be without purpose or effect. God is ready to do something new in your life and your family's life, but you must allow His word to free you from the corrosive effects of the past. The past will eat away at your energy, your joy, and your potential. It will keep you stagnant. Today is your time to spring forward. In chapter 5, will we look at how adversity can create a new beginning.

---

1. Read more (http://en.wikipedia.org/wiki/Hyperthymesia).

2. Parker ES, Cahill L, McGaugh JL (February 2006). "A case of unusual autobiographical remembering." Neurocase 12 (1): 35–49. doi:10.1080/13554790500473680. PMID 16517514

Chapter 5

Suddenly

*She is not afraid of the snow for her household;
for all her household are clothed with scarlet.*
Proverbs 31:21

NO MATTER WHO YOU are, one day you will face a "Suddenly" moment. I describe "Suddenly" moments as circumstances that arise out of nowhere and instantly everything you believe in is challenged during these traumatic situations. A *Suddenly* moment could be the loss of a marriage, a child, a close friendship, or a job. These suddenly moments in life do not define us but rather expose what is already in our hearts. You see "Suddenly" moments can be both good and bad. How many times have we heard about the people who win the lottery or inherit vast amounts of money and then within a year they find themselves bankrupt? Instantaneously, they had more money than they needed and by all appearances, their money troubles were over but because they lacked preparation and the skills to manage their wealth, they are now worse off financially. Their sudden windfall of money in and of itself was not a bad thing. However, by instantly acquiring their wealth instead of earning it through work and saving, they missed the development of valuable skills needed to help them manage and keep their fortune. They did not develop management skills such as saving, budgeting and investing. When they lost their fortune, the issue was not the money itself but rather their lack of financial literacy and self-discipline. This is why they could not keep their "sudden" windfall.

Let's contrast this by examining people who appear to be an "overnight" success. They are suddenly thrust in the forefront of their given profession and everyone recognizes their skill. However, when you examine the lives of these people, you will find that many of them have spent years in preparation refining their skill set. Then life presents them with a challenge that they can solve, and they can seize it because of their diligent preparation. A "suddenly" moment catapults them into a new level of success and notoriety. People may never have heard of them but all of a sudden everyone knows their name. Everyone is buying their product or listening to their music. In reality, their "overnight" success required years of diligence, perseverance and hard work to achieve. You see whatever it is you seek in life you can be guaranteed to find it. Jesus told his disciples to **Ask, Seek, Knock** and they would find. Matthew 7:7

In the New Testament book of Acts, we find one hundred and twenty followers of Jesus Christ. They were confused, shaken, fearful and desperately seeking answers that would explain why their Messiah was crucified. Undoubtedly, some of them had seen the resurrected Savior Jesus Christ. Others in the group had not witnessed his physical resurrection but they believed the accounts of Mary and the other disciples. They were not sure what their next step would be. Who would be able to reveal God's plan to them with the clarity that Jesus the Messiah taught? They were frightened of the Roman government and the Jewish establishment which crucified Jesus. Yet, it was their faith in Jesus and his teachings that continued to burn in their hearts. They continued to come together in prayer and fasting. They were united in an upper room obeying the last command Jesus gave them before his ascension. ***"And, being assembled together with them, commanded them that they should not depart from Jerusalem but wait for the promise of the Father, which saith he, ye have heard of me." Acts 1:4***

The Holy Ghost was the promise Jesus was referring to. When they received the Holy Ghost, they received power. We see that on the appointed day, they were united with one purpose and were praying and seeking God and "suddenly" the room shook. In came a mighty rushing wind and the power of the Holy Ghost fell upon all of them. These early disciples did not know exactly how the Holy Ghost would come but they all obeyed Jesus and were in position for their "suddenly." They came into the upper room as a cowardly, frightened group but each one of them left the room empowered by the same power that raised Jesus from the dead. Gone was the fear of man. Gone was the fear of what people would say. Gone was the fear of what the religious establishment would do to them. In an instant, they were "suddenly" transformed into a mighty army that took the teachings of Jesus and revolutionized the world. All this happened in a "suddenly" moment with God.

Throughout history, great men and women have all faced "suddenly" moments. We admire and honor these great people because they did not quit when they faced terrible circumstances, unfair persecution, or even death itself. What did they do? They continued doing what was right. They stood by their convictions of what was the truth. They fulfilled their destiny. As a virtuous woman, you will have to make a choice when confronted with the "suddenly" moments of your life. Will you cower and be destroyed, or will you stand and be victorious? During the writing of this book, I faced one of my greatest challenges. I was pregnant with a child and after I heard the heartbeat I was filled with great anticipation. As soon as I found out I was pregnant I began praying for a healthy baby, easy pregnancy, and delivery. I took care of myself and did everything I could possibly do to nurture this baby that we so desperately wanted.

When I went in for a check-up immediately there were red flags that I was going to miscarry again. I became hysterical and sat in my car unable to drive or move for what seemed like an eternity. For the next few days, I refused to give up hope. I prayed, read scripture, rested and sought out help anywhere I could find it but eventually, I lost the baby. This was our sixth miscarriage and to be honest for me it was one of the most difficult because I knew it was the last time, I would feel the joy of having a precious life growing inside of me. The pregnancy was an ectopic tubal pregnancy which required the removal of my fallopian tube. I had already lost one tube so from that moment on, it became impossible for me to conceive. As I went into surgery that day, I felt such a cloud of heaviness and darkness come over me. Where was God I questioned? Why would He allow this to happen to me? Thoughts such as, "Don't I have enough faith to believe for a miracle!" only compounded my pain.

The days after the surgery, were a haze of anger, disappointment, and grief. People tried to console me, but I would not allow their words to penetrate my heart. During this time, I wanted to give up teaching and preaching. I questioned how I could stand behind a pulpit and teach that God still answers prayer when ours went unanswered? If God wouldn't strengthen my body to allow me to carry a baby, how could I offer anyone else hope for healing? How could I teach about healing? Then one day, as I lay on the couch, I began to read an article based on the life of the Apostle Paul. The Apostle Paul had a miraculous conversion to Christianity after he encountered the Lord Jesus Christ. From that moment on, he committed his life to the preaching of the gospel and as a result suffered many trials such as beatings, imprisonment, being shipwrecked and lost at sea. However, near the end of his life, he was brought to trial before King Agrippa where he made a powerful statement, ***"But none of these things move me, neither count I my life dear unto myself, so that I might finish my course with joy, and the ministry, which I have received of the Lord Jesus, to testify the gospel of the grace of God." Acts 20:24.***

That statement *"none of these things move me"* challenged me to decide if I was going to allow this difficult situation to move me. "Would my unanswered prayer cause me to lose faith in God's Word?" It is easy to believe that God is for you when things are going well. But it is a completely different thing to walk in faith when there is darkness around you, and you don't understand why you are going through difficulties and challenges. It is also during these times that we can exercise great faith because there is no natural reason to continue to trust God or the Bible. We can determine to cling to an eternal, spiritual hope in Christ and the everlasting life He offers when there is no physical evidence to prove it exists. It is when we step into this realm, that the gift of faith carries us through the darkest hours.

The gift of faith opens our heart so that the Holy Spirit can comfort and strengthen us to continue.

He opens our eyes to the fact that there is hope beyond what we can see today. I began to realize that the devil wanted nothing more than to take this situation and use it to keep me from finishing my course with joy. He wanted to use it to keep me from finishing this book; keep me from sharing the good news with other women that there is hope after disappointments. But the Holy Spirit reminded me that God is faithful to His Word therefore I must always keep my eyes on His Word and not my circumstances. The circumstances of life do not confirm or deny the reality of who God says He is. It is during these "suddenly" events of life that our faith is truly tested.

I have found that during those moments of sorrow, grief, and despair there came a point where I had to choose to allow God to heal my brokenness. I could no longer wallow in the pain of disappointment. Deep inside I knew that if I didn't release the grief and anger, I felt, these emotions would consume me and destroy my dreams. As I read the article that afternoon, I decided to take a step towards freedom. I got up from the sofa with renewed determination to finish my course in life with joy. I resolved to share our story with other couples to offer encouragement and help them. I also decided to become the best children's Sunday School teacher Sister Anna could be. The children that God sent into my class were going to know that God loved them and when they stepped into my classroom, they were going to find a place where His presence could be felt at a very young age. I determined to channel all the love I have for my six children that are waiting for me in heaven into the life of any child I meet while I am here on earth. This is how I can Look at the Future and Laugh.

Let's take a close look at an example of a "suddenly" moment found in the bible. It is the story of a woman whose life was caught off guard by death. She found herself in financial ruin as a result of her husband's death and was desperate to pay off her debt so that her sons would not be taken into slavery. ***Now there cried a certain woman of the wives of the sons of the prophets unto Elisha, saying, "Thy servant my husband is dead, and thou knowest that thy servant did fear the Lord. and the creditor is come to take unto him my two sons to be bondsmen." 2 Kings 4:1***

We find this nameless widow alone and in debt. Gone is her dream of living her life with her husband by her side. Her identity is shattered; she is no longer the prophet's wife. Now she is a poor widow on the verge of losing what she loves the most, her two sons. Everything that provided financial and emotional stability in her life is gone. We do not know how her husband fell into debt or how he died. The Bible only gives us a glimpse of the trauma she experienced; her overwhelming grief was compounded by the fact that she was also in financial ruin. She did all that she could to pay off the debt. She sold her most treasured possessions and even begged the creditor for mercy but there was none to be found. She realized it was only a matter of time before the creditor enslaved her sons. She was desperate knowing that if her sons were enslaved, she would be destitute for the rest of her life. In her society, there were few opportunities for women to work and support themselves.

I imagine that she remembered the day her husband signed the creditor's promissory note. She recalled the apprehension she felt because she knew that her sons could be forced into slavery if they defaulted. She understood that the legal system in Israel would not allow her to declare bankruptcy. If she could not pay the creditor, her sons would become slaves for the next 49 years. If her sons were taken as slaves, her grandchildren would be born slaves and doomed to a life of poverty. Her future looked dark, so she had to make a choice and take decisive action. She sought an answer from God. She knew God would provide direction through his prophet Elisha. When she approached Elisha, he calmly listened to her explain her dilemma. He didn't respond with sympathy and join in a pity party. Instead in an almost callous manner, he asked her two simple but poignant questions: "What shall I do for you? What do you have in the house?"

Wasn't the answer to both of those questions obvious to everyone who knew her situation? She was a poor widow with nothing, and she needed money to pay off the debt. How could he ask her what she had in her house? There was nothing in her house. Gone were the dreams, the laughter, and joy she once felt in her home. Death had come and taken the love of her life. But before she replied, she pondered for a moment and quickly took a mental inventory of what was left in her house. She replied, **"Thine handmaid hath not anything in the house save a pot of oil." 2 Kings 4:2** It was a small jar of oil that she used to anoint her husband's body for his burial. It was precious to her and was the only remaining item of value that she owned. **Then he said, "Go, borrow thee vessels abroad of all thy neighbors; even empty vessels; borrow not a few. And when thou art come in, thou shalt shut the door upon thee and upon thy sons, and shall pour out into all those vessels, and thou shalt set aside that which is full." 2 Kings 4:3-4**

After the widow identified the oil in her possession, the prophet replied with a command that seemed even more outrageous than his original questions. The prophet instructed her to go and borrow as many vessels as she could get a hold of. Imagine going to your neighbors, friends, and family members and asking them to let you borrow their biggest pots, kettles, or anything you could pour oil into. You know they looked at her and asked what she was up to. I know my neighbors would have immediately asked me if I was making tamales. But her response must have seemed awkward, *"I'm not sure why I need them, the prophet Elisha just told me to borrow as many vessels I could get my hands on, so can I borrow your pot?"* She had to take action, obey the instruction and stay in faith to receive from God. (**2 Chronicles 2:20 Believe in the LORD your God, so shall ye be established; believe his prophets, so shall ye prosper.** The Bible states that faith comes by hearing. Romans 10:17 I believe her faith grew every time the widow knocked on someone's door because she had to repeat this request and continued to explain over and over again. "I don't know why I have to borrow vessels. I just know that I'm facing bankruptcy and this prophet has given me hope. I have to obey to receive my miracle." She might have been ridiculed by her neighbors. They may have even said she lost her mind, but instead of going crazy, her faith was growing. Her faith would bring the manifestation of all she believed for. Her actions were a testament that she trusted God as her source, her provider, and her deliverer. Once she gathered as many pots as she could find, she went home and closed the door behind her. She was closing the door to poverty, lack, fear, bondage, people's opinions, and her way of doing things. She was separating herself from the past by immersing herself into the presence of God, Jehovah

Jireh. ***"Pour out into all those vessels, and thou shalt set aside that which is full" 2 Kings 4:4***

Elisha told her to pour into the jars. He didn't say, gather the vessels and call me and I'll go over, and I'll fill them. No, she had to pour the oil out herself. Why? She needed to exercise her faith and trust God for herself. This woman had to take the oil she had in one jar and pour it out in faith. As long as she kept pouring into empty vessels, the oil kept flowing. Many times, we think we can't pray for ourselves. We want to ride on the faith of our Pastors, leaders, parents or others. I am not suggesting that you never reach out to people and ask for prayer. But there comes a point where every person must stand on their own faith. We must pour out the oil for ourselves and trust God as our source.

God will meet any need we have by multiplying what we yield to Him. Even though this woman was desperate, she was obedient. She surrendered herself and was willing to do something about her situation. She didn't just wish that things would get better. God will meet us every time we stop wishing and jump into doing something to change our condition. He will multiply your talents; He will anoint your efforts. God will prosper your ways if you are willing to empty what you have so that He can pour His power into your life. The famous British "Prince of Preachers" Charles Spurgeon as he was known made this commentary: "She was herself to measure out what she should have; and I believe that you and I, in the matter of spiritual blessings from God, have more to do with the measurement of our mercies than we think. We make our blessings little because our prayers are little". (Charles Spurgeon) Did you capture the power in that last statement by the renowned Rev. Spurgeon? "We make our blessings little because our prayers are little". I don't know about you, but I want God to have free course in my life. We need a mighty move of God in our families, communities, and our nation. Pray big prayers. Ask the Father.

So, the Oil Ceased:

As long as this woman poured into empty vessels, the oil continued. Notice the oil wasn't just free flowing. It was being poured out into prepared vessels. The vessels were in the proper position to be filled. The supply of oil was not limited. The oil stopped flowing when there were no more vessels to fill. God's grace is abundantly available to us. His hand is not limited. He's not running out of anything we need. For us to be filled with God's Spirit, we must empty our hearts before Him. We must empty ourselves from pride, anger, unbelief, and anything contrary to His ways. God cannot fill hearts that are filled with the world's ideologies. Often, we limit what God can do for us because we stop utilizing our faith to tap into His plans. We see Him taking care of certain areas of our lives and we become satisfied and so we stop pouring or seeking his power for other things.

It's like us saying yes, God I believe you exist. Yes, God, I believe that when I die because I trust in your Son Jesus as Lord, I will go to heaven but I'm not sure you care about my needs here on earth at this moment. Do you see that? We empty our vessels before Him for salvation, but we carry our very heavy "cares of this world" vessel all by ourselves and He cannot pour His power into those types of vessels. There is no room for His oil in it. The oil only ceased after she stopped pouring into clean, prepared vessels. Don't limit what God can do in your life. Trust Him to pour His loving oil into every area of your life. We can only do that by closing the door behind us and getting into His presence so that the Holy Spirit can cleanse us through the power that is found in the Word of God. This cleansing process requires studying God's Word, praying, fasting and tuning into what He will speak to your heart. As we empty ourselves, He can pour out and fill our lives with His power. **Then she came and told the man of God. And he said, "Go, sell the oil and pay your debt; and you and your sons live on the rest." Vs.7**

She did what she was commanded to do: she did it in faith, and the result answered the end. God takes care to deliver his servants in ways that exercise their faith. He would not have them be little in faith, for faith is the wealth of the heavenly life." (Spurgeon) The reason Spurgeon stated that faith is the wealth of the heavenly life is because faith is what we must present to God for Him to act on our behalf. It does not matter what financial situations we can encounter; God can supply it through faith. God is a Spirit, so any type of money or currency is of no value in the spirit realm. But there is something more powerful than money, gold, silver or precious metals. It is the force of faith. Faith is what pleases God. Hebrews 11:6.

Therefore, when we learn to please God by operating in faith in His Word, then we can tap into the wealth of the heavenly life. Heavenly life is not limited due to circumstances. Heavenly life is not restricted due to economic downturns or geography. A person living in a heavenly life can trust God to provide in any place. Take for example this woman. We don't know what the economy was like for the rest of the community where she was living. But the prophet gave her specific instructions that created a business that flourished just around the corner from the bankruptcy officer that was about to take her boys away. She didn't have to move away to find a better job. She didn't have to compromise her values to find "easy money."

All she had to do was carry out in faith the instructions the prophet had spoken. When it looked like there was no way out of her financial need, God created a business. All she had to do was identify what she had in her home. Then God through the prophet laid out the business plan. It might not have made sense to her, but she started in faith. We need to get to that place where we will flat out obey whatever God is instructing us to do. We can no longer afford to wait to have all the steps 1-2-3 laid out for us before we are willing to step into what God has for us. This is what has limited the church for so long. We need an explanation for everything. God is waiting for empty vessels that are willing to yield the talents and gifts He has given them. He wants to pour out His anointing in your life. Today, it doesn't matter what financial challenges lay before you God hasn't changed. God can open up creative ideas to you. He can turn around seemingly impossible situations. Remember, He cares for you and is ready to pour into empty vessels yielded to Him.

You see many times when we come to God seeking answers to our problems, we expect Him to send some sort of miracle, lightning from heaven, or money from the sky. But oftentimes, I believe God wants us to take an inventory of what we already have in our house. The Bible states that when we have a personal relationship with Jesus Christ His Spirit, the person of the Holy Spirit comes and lives inside of us. Our bodies become "His House." The prophet understood that the best way to help anyone in need was to help them help themselves. This is why he asked her, "what do you have in the house?" If you find yourself in a place of financial need today, ask God through the Holy Spirit to show you what you have in your house.

What talent can you offer the marketplace? What skill can you cultivate that God can bless? To receive a financial breakthrough, just like this widow we must admit that we have a need and we're empty without Him. When we are willing to yield our everyday work to God, He has promised to bless us and enable us to prosper at what we do. Many times, we short-change our talents and abilities. We say things such as "I can only make flower arrangements," not realizing that someone like me is willing to pay top dollar for one of your beautiful arrangements because when it comes to arts and crafts, I have zero skills. I mean if you were to look at one the arrangements that I put together you would know Anna should just stick to writing books and managing her businesses.

What I am trying to say is that everyone has skills and abilities buried within them. Those skills have value in the marketplace. Many people are dissatisfied with their current jobs but are not willing to take the necessary steps to find a new job. They find the process stressful and difficult. If you don't like what you are earning right now, sharpen your skill set. invest the necessary time to find someone that helps you gain more experience. If you aren't making enough money, maybe it is time to find another place of employment. You should take time to accurately assess your strengths and properly market them by writing a good resume. Your financial prosperity is entirely up to you. God has given you talents and abilities. He has revealed spiritual laws that govern prosperity. It is up to us to determine if we are going to follow his direction. What do you have in your house? You see in the Bible oil was a representative of the anointing. King David in the 23rd Psalms paints a picture of the good shepherd anointing oil upon the sheep. This anointing was used to keep bugs from harming the flock. The ointment also helped to heal wounds. If we are to receive anything from God, we must also shut the door behind us and allow the Holy Spirit to anoint us with His Power. *"And it shall come to pass in that day, that his burden shall be taken away from off thy shoulder, and his yoke from off thy neck, and the yoke shall be destroyed because of the anointing." Isaiah 10:27*

A yoke is anything that restricts you and keeps you in bondage. Financial lack is a heavy yoke but God's anointing can destroy any burden, hardship or distressing situation you are facing. We must close the door to our natural way of thinking and stop relying simply on our own abilities. We must close the door to what society says and tune in closely to what the Spirit of God is directing. Many people fail to realize that money is a spiritual matter. They tend to put "religious activities" in a Sunday only compartment, work in a Monday through Friday compartment, family in a separate compartment and money in a completely separate department. But the truth is that your spiritual condition will greatly influence how you manage your money. Jesus said, *"For where your treasure is, there will your heart be also." Mathew 6:21.*

As we've established previously, money is simply a tool. How it is used reflects the spiritual priorities of the manager. Therefore, if you want God's blessing on your vocation and your finances then you must close the door to this world's system of finances and open your heart to the instruction found in the Bible. The world will tell us to buy now pay later. The Bible instructs us to be content with what we have and save for the future. The world system is one of self-indulgence and living for the moment. God's system requires us to trust Him by giving first to God saving and then spending. His system teaches us to save and invest. We are only to spend within our resources. When we are willing to apply these principles in our lives, we begin to experience true financial freedom.

In the next chapter, we are going to study the life of Rahab a prostitute who activated the power of faith to save her family from annihilation and become later known as a champion of faith.

Chapter 6

From Venom to Virtue

*"She fears not the snow for her family,
for all her household are doubly clothed in scarlet"*
Proverbs 31:21

DURING THE WRITING OF THIS book, my husband George and I were asked to be part of a team that was hosting Christmas services at a women's correctional facility in Pennsylvania. I had never been to a correctional facility before, so I was excited and apprehensive about this trip. I wasn't sure what to expect, yet I knew that this was something God wanted us to do. As I prayed and prepared for the trip, I sensed God asking me this question: *"Anna, do you believe that I have found virtuous women, even behind the walls of a state penitentiary?"* I had to ponder if I believed that it would be possible for God to find a virtuous woman serving out a life sentence? Could women who had experienced God's forgiveness and grace walk in the power of His name, even within the confines of a prison cell?

Once I meditated on what God was speaking to my heart, every fear and apprehension lifted from me. I will never forget the joy and true freedom of worship that I sensed during our services. There was such an atmosphere of excitement and love that filled the room where we gathered. These women had prayed for almost two years to have a Christmas service brought to them and God had provided everything necessary. Their worship was not a formality to impress anyone. They weren't being "hyped-up" by fancy religious entertainment. During the services pure, sincere praise was offered up to God for what He had done for them. In spite of the confinement that these women were in, many of them had experienced the forgiveness and true freedom of Jesus and testified about how God changed their lives. Behind prison walls, they found true liberty and were praising God from the depths of their soul. Life had not been easy for them. Many were victims of child abuse, sexual abuse, and domestic violence. So, they turned to drugs, alcohol, and even abusive relationships, to cope with the pain and rejection.

We never asked why they were in prison. It didn't matter. The truth was that none of the regrets, mistakes, or crimes of their past could be changed. We just loved our sisters for who they were that day; members of the body of Christ. When they accepted Jesus Christ, He forgave them of their sins. Regardless of how dark any sin maybe, by the grace of God, anyone can find forgiveness and redemption through the blood of Christ. This change of heart brought hope into their lives. Their eyes were open to see beyond the confinement of the prison bars. They could see themselves as Christ sees them - righteous in His sight. They were in right standing with God and could access His throne through praise and worship. Just like the Virtuous Woman in Proverbs 31, they were no longer fearful. These women no longer feared the future; instead, they discovered that despite the mistakes of their past, there was hope for a better tomorrow. ***"She fears not the snow for her family, for all her household are doubly clothed in scarlet." Proverbs 31:21***

"She fears not" What a powerful statement! You cannot look at the future and laugh with fear in your heart. Notice that this woman recognizes that winter is coming. In literature, winter always symbolizes bareness, hibernation, coldness, despair, and even death. But even in the face of difficult circumstances, this woman fears not. Why? She, along with her family, is prepared for it. How did she prepare for it? They are doubly clothed in scarlet. We are going to examine the life of Rahab, an Old Testament prostitute, to find out what it means to be clothed in scarlet.

When we first encounter Rahab, her country is in turmoil and on the brink of war. Rumors were rampant throughout the city about a small, but peculiar army advancing toward Jericho. What made this nomadic army so frightful, were the unconventional war strategies they deployed. These people had been slaves for more than four hundred years. Their men had no formal military training. Yet, everyone knew that the Hebrew people had conquered every nation that opposed them, including the mighty Egyptian army, the world's super-power at that time. When it seemed like the Egyptians had cornered the Hebrews between the desert and the Red Sea, their God had miraculously parted the sea wide open, allowing 3 million Israelites to cross over into the other side of the desert. Then, as the Egyptian army pursued them into the dry path, the supernatural force that held back the powerful walls of water gave way and every one of the soldiers and their chariots drowned at sea.

As this tribe made its way across the desert, many people in the city of Jericho were growing fearful of an attack. Jericho was a fortified city protected by high walls that surrounded it. For generations, those walls, which measured 54 feet high by 24 feet wide, stood solid and indestructible. The wall's height gave the watchmen a strategic vantage point. Any enemy that attempted to penetrate through the wall was immediately spotted and destroyed. These people continued with their lives; completely trusting a defense mechanism that would soon collapse around them.

Although Rahab found herself in the middle of all of these people, she was not like them. She was held captive by a lifestyle of prostitution. We don't know how she got there. But, just like many women today who find themselves in similar circumstances, it must have involved a painful series of events. Her house was built on those impermeable walls: walls that separated her from an acceptable society. Walls that were insurmountable for her to escape from. She would never be able to climb down from them and live among "respectable" people. Everyone knew what she did for a living. She couldn't imagine herself married to a loving husband. *"Who would ever want a woman who sold her body to others as a wife,"* she reasoned. Men came to the walls of the city, in the dark of night, so that they wouldn't be seen coming to her to fulfill their sexual lust. She knew them all: rich, powerful, religious, family men, poor men, and strangers alike.

On the surface, these men each seemed different. But everything she had been through taught her to believe all men were the same. They were all driven to her by lust. To them, she was nothing more than an object to be used. It was nothing but business. There seemed to be no escape for Rahab; until the day she heard of the supernatural acts of the Hebrew's God. Rahab knew that if what she had heard about their God was true, her city would be destroyed. The walls would offer no protection and everything that brought safety and security to Jericho would be demolished. The streets had hardened Rahab's heart. She had been violated and victimized over and over again. But this time, as destruction loomed near, she would not sit back defenseless; waiting for anyone to save her. After all, she was a survivor and she would find a way to rescue her family.

One day, two spies came to her house seeking, not sexual favors, but shelter. Rahab immediately recognized that there was something different about them. It wasn't their physical appearance, but something deeper. It was nothing that could be described but; rather, it was sensed. They walked with assurance and inner strength. Although they saw the high walls, they were not intimidated by them. They were not frightened by Jericho's army or the watchmen that stood on the walls ready to defend the city. They were on a mission and nothing was going to stand in their way. When Rahab saw the spies, she knew for certain that the city was doomed for destruction.

While others panicked in fear, Rahab saw an opportunity to escape the bondage that she found herself in and a chance to start her life over again. There were many other lodges along the Jericho wall; how was it that these two spies came to her? Was it just a coincidence? Could their God have seen the faith that was springing within Rahab's heart and directed the spies to her? Was it possible that their God was showing mercy towards a woman everyone else had discarded? This was Rahab's moment to seek the truth, and so she quickly let the two spies into her lodge. She knew her every move was being watched so she would have to take quick, decisive action to plead for her life and the lives of her family. Once they were inside, Rahab told them all that she had heard about the God of Israel. She told them how the entire city was full of fear and they were terrified of facing the Israelite army. Just then, the King of Jericho sent his messengers and demanded that Rahab turn over these men, who were seen entering into her lodge. She was faced with a decision. Would she remain captive to her current situation and give in to the king's demand or would she take a step of faith and collaborate with the spies? Destruction was imminent and she was at a crossroads. At that moment, Rahab demonstrated her faith in their God by turning her back on the idols of Jericho. She chose to hide the spies and send the king's men that sought them in a different direction. When her allegiance was proven to the spies, Rahab proposed a deal: ***"Now therefore, I pray you, swear unto me by the Lord, since I have shewed you kindness, that ye will also shew kindness unto my father's house, and give me a true token: And that ye will save alive my father, and my mother, and my brethren, and my sisters, and all that they have, and deliver our lives from death."***

    They agreed to her request and formed a pact, stating that when they came to destroy Jericho, her home, and everyone inside of it, would be spared. However, this pact was conditioned upon two things: one that she would not reveal their plans to anyone and second that she tie a scarlet cord in the window, through which she let them in. A period of time past between when the spies left Jericho and when they returned with the army to attack Jericho. During this time, Rahab gathered her extended family into her home. She persuaded them to trust in the God of Israel for freedom. While fear and uncertainty filled the people of Jericho, hope arose within her every time she heard others talk about the God of the Israelites. As the army marched across the desert and grew closer to the city, tension filled the air. The people of Jericho, young and old alike were stricken with fear and they reassured themselves that they would be protected within the great walls.

Then, one day, the most peculiar thing occurred. When the army finally reached Jericho, instead of launching a full-force attack, they simply marched around the entire perimeter of the city one time. The only sound that could be heard came from the trumpets blown by their priests. Not one of their soldiers said a word. Their general neither issued an order nor called for Jericho to surrender. They just marched. This pattern continued for six days. They came and marched around the city one time. With each passing day, the citizens of Jericho grew more and more terrified. The soldiers simply marched in silence. The only sounds that were heard were sounds of praise coming from the trumpets.

We can learn from this. God was the one who designed this military strategy. He was the original creator of psychological warfare. From the natural, this plan seemed foolish. At any moment, the watchmen could have attacked this vulnerable nomadic army from on top of the wall. They could have shot arrows at them, but they didn't. God's plan demanded that the soldiers march in silence, relying completely on the Lord for protection, without saying a word. I believe that the reason they had to march in silence was to quench doubt and unbelief. While studying their journey into the Promised Land we see that God wanted to deliver Jericho into their hands 40 years prior. Moses had sent twelve spies into this very city to explore the land. However, the negative words of ten spies brought fear into the hearts of three million people and none of them lived to enter into the Promised Land. Joshua and Caleb were the only two spies who believed that God could help them conquer the giants of the land.

They were the lone survivors of that generation. Therefore, when Joshua was Commander of Israel, he did things differently. He only sent in two spies to scout the land. I believe that God commanded the soldiers to remain silent so that their words would not cancel out their faith. When we believe that God will act on our behalf, we must place a guard over our mouth. Our words must line up with His promises. You can't say you trust that God is your provider and then go around talking lack, poverty, and insufficiency. If you can't speak faith-filled words, then follow God's proven warfare plan and simply keep your mouth closed. If you can't speak words of faith, then don't say anything at all. Don't speak of the giants and obstacles. Just silently worship and meditate on God's faithfulness. God was ready to bring them into their destiny 40 years earlier but their fear and doubt delayed the fulfillment of His plan. God is ready to work on your behalf now if you simply say what He can do about your situation.

When the seventh day arrived, the army marched around the city; not once, twice, or three times, but seven times. As Rahab saw the army marching around the city, she had to maintain her faith in the promise that the spies made to her. It was time to make sure her entire family was in her house. Tensions mounted as the army continued its march. Then, as they started their seventh round, the silence was shattered when the soldiers shouted a declaration of praise and the walls all around the city instantaneously crumbled. The soldiers rushed in and Rahab watched in amazement as the city was completely overtaken. She and those found within the four walls of her home were saved, because of her faith and her obedience.

The scarlet cord was hanging on her window. When destruction came to Jericho, the God of Israel brought salvation and removed the venom of sin from the life of Rahab. The walls of Jericho collapsed around her and she was freed from the bondage that had identified her. In Jericho, she was Rahab, the prostitute; however, amongst the Israelites and generations to come she was named among the champions of faith. God honored her faith in Him and the scarlet cord she hung on her window was a symbol of the blood of Jesus that was shed on the cross. The scarlet cord would remove the shame of her past and brought them into a promised land. The Bible tells us that Rahab later married Salmon, a wealthy Israelite leader. Rahab is listed in the genealogy of Jesus because she was the great grandmother of King David. ***"You see that a person is justified by works and not by faith alone. Likewise, was not Rahab the prostitute also justified by works when she welcomed the messengers and sent them by another road? For just as the body without the spirit is dead, so faith without works is dead." James 2:24-26***

What about you? Maybe your life hasn't always been perfect and you've had a rough childhood. Maybe you have been sexually, physically, or emotionally abused and you feel rejected by society. The enemy has come against you and tried to destroy your self-esteem and self-worth. You have built up walls around to you keep you from feeling the shame and humiliation. Today, there is hope. That hope comes from realizing that your past does not determine your future. What others say about you cannot keep you tied to your failures. Through faith in Jesus Christ, you can tear down the walls of regret, guilt, shame, and fear. These negative emotions are like venom in your soul. Venom is a toxin that destroys its victims by paralyzing them and numbing them, to the point of suffocation. However, a victim can survive a venomous bite if antivenom is given to them.

The anti-venom takes away the deadly effects of a poisonous sting, although the scar of the bite might remain. The pain is lifted and life has been restored. In the same manner, the devil is often referred to as a serpent throughout the Bible. Because of Adam's disobedience, sin entered the world and separated us from God. This disobedience opened the door to both natural physical death and eternal death, or separation from God. In Romans 6:23 we are told, **"For the wages of sin is death; but the gift of God is eternal life through Jesus Christ our Lord."** The only way to restore a relationship with a perfect God is through Jesus' death. When Jesus came to earth, He was exposed to the sting, or venom, of sin. He was perfect, but, on the cross, the sins of all humanity were laid on Him. He died and paid the wages of sin by going to hell on our behalf. However, Jesus rose from the dead; meaning the devil could not keep Him in hell. **"O death, where is your victory O death, where is your sting." I Corinthians 15:55**

You no longer have to be fearful of death. Why? When you place your faith in the blood of Jesus, death cannot destroy you. The moment Jesus forgives your sins, you start a new life. You can look at your future knowing that God has good things planned for you. The scar, or memory, of your past, will remain, but it can no longer haunt or destroy you. You too can have the venom in your life turned into virtue. Look at Rahab. In the New Testament, she is one of only four women listed in the genealogy of Jesus Christ. She is even mentioned in the book of Hebrews "Who's Who" Hall of Faith. She is referred to as Rahab, the prostitute, but the reason her past is even mentioned is not to shame or disgrace her, but rather to show us that her faith opened the door for God to work through her, regardless of her sinful condition. When we cry out to Him in faith, God will respond no matter how desperate our situation. He sent his spies to her house. Her brave actions demonstrated faith in God, and He rewarded her by giving her a new beginning.

When her countrymen were talking fear, destruction, and doom, she changed her mindset. She spoke faith-filled words of protection, provision, and a fresh start. How do I know this? She trusted in the pact that she made with the spies and immediately hung the scarlet cord on her window- where it could be seen. That scarlet cord was a symbol of her trust in Jehovah. Despite her reputation, she cared for her family and told them that God would deliver them. She was not satisfied to escape the destruction alone. Instead, she pulled her father, mother, brothers, sisters and their children into her house. They would no longer fear what was head because they were covered by the scarlet cord. They were in the household of faith. Her own family may have rejected her, hurt her but yet Rahab still demonstrated that she had a loving and caring heart. She sought salvation for her family. They would have a new beginning.

We live in a time when many people are fearful. They see how things are very uncertain in our economy, the world markets, and even nature itself. When they see the increased number of severe storms, earthquakes, and natural disasters, people wonder what is causing them. These events are calling our attention to the fact that something in the spirit realm is about to shift. Now is the time for us to walk out our faith in Jesus Christ and look for His return. Just like Rahab, we need to pull our families closer together and make sure they are covered by the scarlet cord of redemption. If you are a believer and God wants to reach your family through your voice. If there has been strife or rejection within your family in the past, allow the Holy Spirit to heal your heart and release forgiveness. Your family needs you to be a channel by which the message of salvation can reach them. Do not allow the enemy to keep you locked in a prison of pain and unforgiveness but rather choose to be a messenger of hope. While everyone around her feared, Rahab carried a message of deliverance. Rahab a prostitute became an evangelist to her family. Her message was urgent, and she spoke with boldness because she was confident that God would protect them. When she told her family about the pact she made with the spies, it brought faith to them and they turned to God for protection.

Things all around us may look uncertain, but for the Christian, they are just signs that our redemption is closer. We don't have to fear what is ahead because our hearts are clothed in scarlet. The power of the blood of Jesus protects us. Now is the moment to call others into the glorious household of faith. The world systems that many people trust will be collapsing but you carry the message of hope within you. The scarlet cord hanging from the window of our heart demonstrates our total dependence upon the Lord. He can deliver us from every situation we will ever face. He has promised to never leave us nor forsake us. He can give us a new beginning no matter what circumstance comes against us. In our next chapter, we will study the life of Naomi. Her journey is marked by great loss and mourning. She returns to her homeland empty and depleted but discovers her restoration while helping a young woman find her place in history.

Chapter 7

Finding Hope

*Her husband is known in the gates,
when he sitteth among the elders of the land.*
Prov. 31:23

FUNERALS... THE VERY WORD conjures up memories of pain and grief. At one time or another; we have all attended them to show our respect for a deceased friend or relative. Funerals allow us to celebrate the life of the departed and offer our emotional support to their family, without fully understanding the immensity of their grief. We will go back to our normal routine, but these grieving loved ones will have to learn how to cope with life without their spouse, child, parent, or grandparent. Nothing will ever be the same and there is no way to turn back time. There is no way to have even just one more day. We've all heard the cries *"If I could only talk to them one more time."* It's the voice of profound longing and lament. For some people, the voice springs out of with regret. They regret the call that they did not place; the bitterness that they chose to harbor toward that person; the words of love and gratitude that they left unspoken.

Yet, other people yearn to speak with their loved ones, because of the joy that person imparted. Their loved one was a source of strength, security, and the blessing of knowing that someone was in their corner; someone loved them unconditionally. Death, for many people, is final. There is the hopelessness that comes from knowing that no amount of prayer is going to change things. There is no way to "fix" death. After a funeral, all that remains is the bleakness of having to continue to live your life without them in it.

The first time the word "hope" is mentioned in the Bible, it is spoken by a broken and grieving widow named Naomi. ***"If I should say I hope, if I should have a husband tonight and bear sons, would you wait for them until they were grown? Would you restrain yourselves from having husbands? No my daughters; for it grieves me for your sakes that the hand of the Lord has gone against me." Ruth 1:12-13*** Naomi's life was marked with tragedy and sorrow. In the book of Ruth, she finds herself a widow; destitute and homeless in a foreign land. When we first meet her, she is dealing with the pain that no mother would wish upon another- the loss of, not one, but both of her sons within 24 months. She is utterly alone in a foreign country, with nothing but the clothes on her back. She has no husband and no means of supporting herself. In her culture, women were not viewed as equal to men and they had to rely on a husband or sons for their livelihood. Naomi realized that, at her age and residing in an enemy country, all hope for finding another man with whom she could build a life again was gone.

Often, in the loneliness of night, she reflected on the days when she and her husband, Elimelech, enjoyed the comforts of life in Bethlehem. They were both seen as outstanding community leaders with many friends and acquaintances; everyone in the city knew them. Naomi was widely regarded as a pleasant woman, exactly as her name denoted. She was well-respected, because of her kindness and concern for those she came in contact with. She could still vividly recall the joy on Elimelech's face whenever he was with their two young sons, Mahlon and Chilion. They were his pride and joy and he would do anything to provide for his family. With Elimelech by her side, Naomi felt protected and complete. They married young and had worked hard to build a better life for their family. If you would have told her that one day she would find herself completely alone and adrift in a pagan land, she would have never believed you. After all, they were good people and certainly, God would not allow bad things to come upon good people.

Everything in Naomi's life was going well until the famine hit. Elimelech did everything he could to keep the crops alive. He and the boys worked from the crack of dawn until late every night, watering the fields and looking for new pastures for their animals. She planted their homestead garden that summer, just as she had so many years before, hoping that the harvest would be plentiful enough to hold them through the winter. However, this year was different- the drought scorched their entire crop. All of her efforts yielded nothing, and what wasn't scorched, was destroyed by an infestation. Then, slowly they watched as their animals began to starve and die from dehydration. Times were hard everywhere, so Elimelech decided to leave the family homestead. That decision was one of the most gut-wrenching choices they had ever made.

The land had been in their family for generations. Their farm had always produced more than enough for them to survive. Now, it seemed as though heaven itself had closed its windows, and there was no rain. How did things get so bad? Elimelech, whose name meant My God is King, was once confident and full of life. He walked with his head up and his body exuded strength, as he took his seat with the elders along the city gates. Elimelech was a moral man who followed God, as best he could, and he always tried to do the right thing. Now, he looked like a defeated old man. There was nothing he could do for himself, his family, or the people of Bethlehem. Day after day, he left early in the morning, hoping to find food only to come back empty-handed. Naomi tried to encourage him but no way of supporting his family, Elimelech quickly sunk into a hole of depression. It seemed as though his heart became as hardened as the cracked soil that had once produced a bountiful harvest.

He was dry inside and anger quickly filled his heart with despair. The drought didn't just last one year, but it continued to the next, and soon, famine was all around them. People were dying, children were malnourished. How could this be happening in Bethlehem, in a city whose very name meant "House of Bread?" Jehovah had always provided for Bethlehem. It was a peaceful community that was full of abundance. In those years of plenty and prosperity, the priest warned the people not to forget Jehovah and honor Him, but slowly, one generation at a time, they walked away from God. Jehovah was no longer the center of their focus and many of them weren't sure they even needed God. They were hard-working people who began to think they could handle things on their own, without depending on the religious tales of their parents.

Then, one day, out of sheer desperation, Elimelech formulated a plan to take things into his own hands. He would no longer sit and wait for Jehovah to "miraculously" rescue his family. "Where is Jehovah now?" he questioned. He knew that the famine was a punishment from God, but why did everyone have to suffer? What had he and his family done to deserve this? Eventually, he gave into to a once unthinkable action. To find work, he decided to move his family to Moab. He heard there was food there and was willing to make the 130-mile journey. Many people tried to dissuade Elimelech from leaving.

They told him to trust God and see how God would, once again, remember Bethlehem and restore it to its former glory. Yet, in Elimelech's mind, God had not been King. All he could see was blight, despair, and charred ruins of what had been. He wondered how there could ever be a better future for his sons in this place. Once the decision was made, Naomi saw a glimpse of hope in Elimelech's eyes. Yet, how could she agree to move her family to Moab? The Moabites were sworn enemies of Israel She knew that the Moabites were the descendants of Lot's incestuous relationship with his daughter and that they practiced the pagan worship of Chemosh; which included the brutal ritual of human sacrifice. Her sons were now young men; how would they find suitable wives, if they left Bethlehem?

Naomi found herself torn between having to decide whether to follow Elimelech, the love of her life or try to persuade him to stay and trust the God of their people. When Elimelech would not change his mind, she rationalized that things would be OK. They were only doing what was best for their sons and God would be with them, even in Moab. When they finally arrived at Moab, things were exactly as Elimelech said they would be. The marketplace was full of vendors selling fresh fruits and vegetables. Her eyes feasted on the vibrant colors and smell of the abundant produce, milk, and honey that was everywhere. At that moment, all of their troubles were nothing but a distant memory in a faraway land. They would just keep to themselves and not intermingle with the Moabites. Elimelech assured her that they could still worship Jehovah in the privacy of their home. He was convinced that their boys would not be influenced by their pagan environment and that they would follow after the faith of their forefathers.

The Bible doesn't give us specifics on how and when Elimelech died in Moab, but we are told that his sons grew, and eventually, inter-married with Moabite women. Although Naomi grieved the death of her husband, she took comfort in the fact that she still had her boys. They were young and strong and promised to take care of her. Then, the unthinkable happened, and once again, Naomi found herself standing next to the coffin of her son. Her life seemed like a nightmare that she could not wake up from. First, they lost their home in Bethlehem. Then, she lost her husband, followed by her son, Mahlon.

Her heart was broken and bleeding from within. The days seemed to all blend from one right into the next. She simply went through the motions of survival, but there was little joy left inside of her. Naomi was supported by her sole surviving son, Chilion and her two daughters-in-law, Ruth and Orpah. In her grief, she didn't notice how her son was growing pale and weak, until the day that she heard a loud screech coming from the house. She ran inside and found her daughter-in-law slumped over the body of her dead husband. Orpah called out to her god, Chemosh, in anguish and despair, but Naomi simply stood frozen unable to process what had just happened. She couldn't cry; she couldn't scream; she couldn't run. Her world completely collapsed around her. She stood over the grave of the only thing she had left to live for, her one surviving son. Without her husband and her sons, she was left depleted and destitute. Where could she go next?

She left the drought of Bethlehem to find food in the land of her enemies. Yes, her family found the material things that they needed to survive, but now she was parched and thirsting for something that could not be satisfied with mere food and drink. She was empty. In her state of grief, the only thing that remained alive within her was a deep desire to return home. She heard that God had once again visited Bethlehem and she yearned to be sheltered within the walls of her people. All that was important to her was gone, so she determined to walk the long treacherous journey again.

She had nothing left to lose, and out of her deep desperation, a strange sense of fearlessness was birthed. Out of the darkness of grief and sorrow, slowly, a glimmer of hope began to shine. Ten years prior, Naomi would have never even considered walking through 130 miles of desert land by herself alone and defenseless. She could rely on Elimelech and her boys to protect her then, but now she had no one. Surely, she could not expect Ruth or Orpah to leave their families and country to follow her. She had nothing to offer them. The custom of their day would have allowed the girls to marry another surviving brother so that the family name could continue, but Naomi was well past childbearing. There would never be another son. Naomi loved her daughters-in-law but knew the time had come for her to release them and allow them to live their own lives. They were still young and beautiful, with plenty of life before them. They would be fine to return to their families.

As each day passed, Naomi found more and more comfort in the thought of returning to Bethlehem. She wasn't sure if she could make it back to Bethlehem alive, but deep in her heart, she knew she had to set out. She would no longer wallow in her grief, trapped in Moab, by a pit of anger, fear, and despair. She was determined to get back to God. It was a matter of survival. Yes, she decided to take this journey, even though her heart was broken, bleeding with pain, and filled with sorrow. Many nights she found herself restless, asking the same questions, over and over again, *"Why God, why?"* What had they done to deserve all of this tragedy? Why was God so angry with her? She remembered their decision to move to Moab and could not shake the image of all three of her strong men lying in their coffins within ten years. It was a decade of tremendous loss, and at times, it was too much to bear. Yet, despite her grief, she knew it was time to go back to the land of her forefathers. She could not change the past, but she had to return home and rebuild a life for herself. The next morning, when the daylight finally arose,

Naomi gathered her daughters-in-law, Orpah, and Ruth, to her side. She told them how she loved them as her own daughters. The grief and sorrow they experienced bound their hearts together in a way few people understood. They all loved strong, honest, and good men, only to have them taken away. Now, there was nothing left for Naomi in Moab. She explained her plan to return to her homeland, Bethlehem. She did not want to become a burden for Orpah or Ruth. Naomi's plan stunned them; it was unimaginable to even think about separating from her. They loved her and felt compassion for her, but Naomi would not be dissuaded. She was leaving for Bethlehem and they would never see her again. As Naomi walked out of the door, she turned and spoke a blessing over them. ***"...the Lord deal kindly with you, as you have dealt with the dead and with me. The Lord grant you that ye may find rest, each of you in the*** *house of her husband." Ruth 1:8-9* She gently kissed each one on the cheek and they wept uncontrollably. They rushed behind her, trying to pull her back into the security of their home. "We will return with you to your people," they pledged. Yet, Naomi insisted they return to their families. She had nothing to offer, and out of sheer frustration, she exclaimed, *"Turn again, my daughters go your way for I am too old to have an husband. If I should say, I have hope, if I should have an husband also to night, and should also bear sons. Would ye tarry for them till they were grown? Would ye stay for them from having husbands? Na, my daughers; for it grieveth me much for your sakes that the hand of the Lord is gone out against me." Ruth 1:12-13*

At that moment, all of the rage and bitterness that was bottled inside of her spewed out from the depths of her soul, as she declared that God had turned His face against her. There was no easy answer or a good explanation for all the pain and suffering she experienced. She knew that Jehovah God was angry with her, and He alone, was responsible for all of her family's troubles. How could she expect either Orpah or Ruth to follow her God into a future of continued uncertainty? *"Go back,"* she urged, *"Go back to your families, your traditions, your gods and your people."* Each woman stood at a crossroads, stunned with Naomi's declaration, and yet, they all realized that this was a moment that would set their destiny. This decision would change their lives forever.

Orpah knew that Naomi loved her. As she looked into Naomi's tired and lonely eyes, she understood that if she moved to Bethlehem, then one day, she too might find herself alone in a foreign land. Yes, her first reaction was to pledge to go with Naomi, but the more she thought about moving to Bethlehem and cutting all ties with Moab, the more she realized that the risk was too great. She could not picture a better life for herself in Bethlehem. Reluctantly, Orpah kissed Naomi good-bye and returned to her people. Naomi understood Orpah's reasoning and turned to release Ruth back to her family. How could she expect either one of them to leave everything? They had fulfilled their marriage vows to her sons. They had no commitment or obligation to care for her. Naomi truly desired the best for them, so she urged Ruth to follow Orpah and begin a new life in Moab.

In that instant, Ruth vividly remembered the day she met Naomi and her family. Although they were foreigners in Moab, she found herself drawn to them. It was as if they brought light into her very dark world. She remembered how they held on to the hope that their God, Jehovah, would someday send a Messiah to deliver them from their oppressors and make Israel a great nation. They spoke of Bethlehem and how it thrived when the hand of the Lord was with them. They longed for the day when they could return, and once again, enjoy the blessing of Jehovah. She saw, in Naomi, an unexplainable strength. Naomi had shown such great love toward her that she could not imagine living the rest of her life without her. Suddenly, with her heart racing, Ruth leapt forward, clung tightly to Naomi and boldly declared her intentions, ***"Entreat me not to leave thee, or to return from following after thee; for whither thou goest, I will go, and where thou lodgest, I will lodge. Thy people shall be my people, and thy God, my God. Where thou diest, will I die, and there I will be buried. Do so to me and more also, if ought but death part thee and me. Ruth 1:16-17***

Naomi marveled at Ruth's commitment and silently thanked the Lord that she would not journey alone. These two heartbroken women would begin their dangerous journey across 130 miles of desert. It would take days for them to make the trip. They would be exposed to brutal heat and frigid nights, attacks from wild animals or thieves and with no man there to protect them. They would start a new life in Bethlehem, with no one to lean on, except each other and their faith in an unseen God, who seemed distant and unresponsive to their prayers. As they walked across that desert, every step was a step of faith. Naomi found herself lost in her thoughts and the desert sand became a large screen that flashed back the memories of her family's journey to Moab. She could see her young boys running ahead of her and Elimelech. The memories seemed so real that she could almost hear their laughter. She recalled the nights around the campfire as she prepared the evening's meal for her boys and the reflection of Elimelch's face as it shone in the glowing wood ambers.

Those were happy times. Abruptly, her thoughts were interrupted and she was, once again, drawn back to the emptiness and loneliness she now felt. She was no longer the hopeful young woman who had journeyed this path ten years ago. Life had not been fair to her and now she was left with a deep bitterness that could not be erased. She was willing to take the risk and walk through the desert, once again, because she didn't care if she survived to see the next day or not. Each new day no longer held the promise of something better; instead, each new day was more time to remember what used to be. Each day was another day to think about what she no longer had.

Finally, after six days of walking through the dry, hot wilderness, Naomi and Ruth caught a glimpse of the outskirts of Bethlehem. Their hearts began to pound as they realized that their destiny was within reach. They knew that their lives would never be the same, but perhaps, Jehovah would be merciful on them and allow them to find happiness once again. The momentary excitement that they felt quickly vanished as they began to imagine, again, what people would think when they arrived. Anxiety and apprehension gripped their minds. How would Naomi explain the great pain, loss, and suffering that she had endured? How would she face her family and friends, now that she came back with nothing? Alone in her thoughts, she fought back the tears of anger and bitterness that she felt. Her heart was as dry as the desert sand that she struggled to walk through, with each step requiring more strength than the last. Bitterness had so gripped her heart that any happiness she experienced was immediately swallowed into the pit of anger deep within her very soul. She was no longer the once pleasant young woman filled with happiness and love. Life had been cruel and unfair to her. She did not deserve the catastrophes that left her heartbroken and resentful, yet she continued trudging forward.

When they finally arrived in Bethlehem, news of their arrival spread quickly. Many of Naomi's friends ran to greet her, but they stood shocked and in disbelief when they saw her. Could this be the same Naomi? She knew what they were thinking. She could see it in their eyes, and before anyone could even ask what happened, she declared, ***"Call me not Naomi, call me Mara for the Almighty has dealt very bitterly with me. I went out full, and the Lord hath brought me home again empty: Why then call ye me Naomi, seeing the Lord hath testified against me, and the Almighty hath afflicted me?" Ruth 1:20-21*** One by one, they awkwardly greeted her. No one knew what to say. They all remembered seeing her leave full and now she returned with nothing but the clothes on her back. She had no husband, no sons, and only Ruth, her heathen daughter-in-law, stood by her side. They were all amazed that this beautiful young woman was willing to leave her country and take care of Naomi.

Early the next morning, Ruth rose and was eager to find work. She was determined to provide for Naomi and herself. They would not become a burden to anyone. This was a strange new country, and although she did not fully understand their customs, she knew that God was with her. He had protected them through the desert, and she was confident that He would guide her to a kind landowner who would allow her to glean in his field. She informed Naomi of her plan and left their home in search of a place where she could harvest enough barley for their next meal. Ruth silently prayed as she journeyed through the roads of Bethlehem. "Please God show me where I can find a kind farmer who will allow me to pick up the grain that is left over from their harvest," she pleaded. Ruth marveled at the beauty of the countryside. It was everything that she imagined it would be; just as Mahon had described it.

They dreamed of the day they would return to his childhood city. Mahon's memory gave her the strength to carry on. As daylight broke, she heard voices of people starting their workday in a bountiful grain field. She stood and watched them for a while and noticed a small band of women harvesting grain and bundling up in sheaves. Immediately, she asked the overseer for permission to gather whatever fell to the ground. She assured him that she would not take from the harvest and would keep her distance from the hired workers. When he asked her what her name was, she replied, "Ruth." Instantly, he knew that she was the Moabite woman everyone was talking about. She and her mother-in-law, Naomi, were both widows, so he could not deny her request, because their law demanded that widows, the poor, and foreigners be allowed to glean in the outer perimeters of the field.

As the morning went by, the overseer kept his eye on Ruth and noticed there was something about her demeanor that was distinctive. Everyone knew she was a proselyte and had come to believe in Jehovah. But many wondered how she could have left her family to worship God and take care of Naomi? In spite of all that she had suffered, she was not consumed with self-pity but was willing to work to support herself. She spoke with a confidence and respectfulness that instantly drew people to her. It was evident, that Ruth was a capable woman; full of dignity and self-respect. After some time, he heard Boaz, the field owner, arriving. Boaz quickly noticed the new young woman gleaning in his field.

"Who is she?" Boaz questioned.

"Ruth, the Moabite," the overseer responded. He continued to describe how Ruth had requested permission to glean in their fields and how she worked diligently from the time that she arrived. Boaz was instantly intrigued. He had heard so much, throughout the city, about this woman. Now, he would take the opportunity to meet her for himself. As he walked toward where she was working, he could not help but notice the delicate features of her face and the smoothness of her youthful skin. Surprisingly, he was instantly drawn to her.

"My daughter," he called out to her. He proclaimed, ***"Do not glean anywhere else but stay and work close to my female servants." Ruth 2:8-9*** As a well-connected landowner, he knew firsthand of the dangers experienced by a young foreign woman working in other areas and wanted to protect her from any cruel treatment or abuse. Without any hesitation, he urged her to work with his maidservants, until both the barley and wheat fields had been harvested. He assured her that she would be protected. Unknown to Ruth, he secretly instructed the overseer to leave extra grain behind and allow her to gather as much as she wanted. He also granted her permission to drink from the clean water that he provided to his field help. When Ruth heard his offer, she became overwhelmed by his generosity. Jehovah had answered her prayers through the kindness of this older man. Instantly, she fell at his feet and thanked him. She knew that Boaz's offer was more than customary. As the tears of gratitude flowed down her face, Ruth humbly asked why he would do this for her- a lowly foreigner. What had she done to deserve so much compassion and goodwill from such a powerful man as Boaz?

His answer astonished her. He explained that he heard how she left her family and country to care for Naomi. He admired the courage that Ruth exhibited by leaving all that she knew to come to a strange country. When it was time for his workers to take their final break, Boaz invited Ruth to join the reapers and eat bread. She slowly savored every morsel of fresh bread dipped in vinegar. She could hardly remember the last time that she was able to eat until she was full. Boaz found himself fighting back the urge to stare at this beautiful young woman. Instead, he awkwardly glanced across the table, careful not to be noticed, as he watched Ruth enjoy the afternoon's meal.

As the day ended, Ruth hurried through the field toward their home in the city. She could hardly wait to show Naomi all of the grain that she had harvested and shared a portion of the lunch that she saved for her. Naomi eagerly greeted Ruth with a kiss. All-day long, she wondered where Ruth would find work. She prayed for God to be with Ruth and lead her to a kind field owner. As soon as she saw Ruth's basket overflowing with grain and bread, she knew her prayers were answered. "Where did you work and get all this food?" Naomi asked. She exclaimed, ***"God bless the man that showed you so much kindness!" Ruth 2:19***

"I worked for a man named Boaz," Ruth responded. Immediately, Naomi remembered that Boaz was one of their wealthy relatives. Ruth told Naomi how he had shown her kindness, by allowing her to drink from the harvester's water and eat with the maidservants and he even instructed that she only glean from his fields, so that she would not be harmed. Naomi encouraged Ruth to continue working in his fields. Secretly, Naomi began to reflect on Boaz's generosity toward Ruth. She would wait to see if his intentions were genuine, before suggesting that he perform the duties of the kinsman-redeemer. The kinsman-redeemer protected the family's honor and defended the weak. If a family member fell into financial hardship, the kinsman-redeemer could pay their debt and claim the land that belonged to their family.

Naomi was wise and she could see God's hand of provision upon Ruth's life. As the harvest season neared completion, Naomi knew that it was the perfect time to ask Boaz to fulfill the role of the kinsman-redeemer. She desired for Ruth to have a man worthy of her kindness and love. The customs of her land prohibited a woman from arranging a marriage for Ruth, but she was determined to find out if Boaz would take Ruth for a bride. During that week, Ruth talked about the night of winnowing that Boaz planned. He would host a large dinner and then he and the fieldsmen would use the night's breeze to separate the grain from the chaff. As Ruth spoke, Naomi formulated a plan.

When the night of winnowing arrived, Naomi instructed Ruth to wash and put on her best clothes. Ruth would then discreetly go to the threshing floor, where Boaz would be working, and not allow anyone to see her. Naomi told her to wait until Boaz fell asleep and then lie at his feet. It was very risky, but Naomi felt that Boaz would fulfill the role of kinsman-redeemer. At around midnight that evening, Boaz was startled, as he awoke to find Ruth lying at his feet. He said, ***"Who art thou? And she answered, I am Ruth thine handmaid; spread therefore thy skirt over thine handmaid: for thou art a near kinsman' " Ruth 3:9*** Boaz could hardly believe what he was hearing. How was it possible that she was coming to him and requesting that he take her in marriage? ***"Blessed be thou of the Lord, my daughter. For thou hast shewed more kindness in the latter end than at the beginning, inasmuch as thou followedst not young men, whether poor or rich." Ruth 3:10***

Boaz was amazed that she was willing to marry a man so much older than her, to maintain the memory of her dead husband's family name in the tribe of Judah. He was moved by her kindness. The entire community spoke of her character and regarded her in high-esteem for her dedication to Naomi and her selfless compassion. Boaz would be proud to have Ruth as his wife. Yes, he was willing to fulfill the role of the kinsman-redeemer, but there was one relative that was a closer relative to Elimelech than he was. Boaz knew that their law required that this man be given the first opportunity to redeem the land and marry Ruth. As they parted ways, to prove his intentions to Naomi, Boaz filled Ruth's shawl with six bushels of barley.

When Ruth returned home, Naomi saw the full shawl and knew that everything had gone well. Naomi could see God moving on behalf of Ruth and she assured her that Boaz would resolve this issue quickly. Boaz gathered the elders of the community and the kinsman. He explained the fact that Naomi was ready to sell the land that belonged to her dead husband and then asked if the relative was ready to assume the role of the kinsman-redeemer. The relative was eager to buy the land until Boaz explained that Naomi was also demanding that the kinsman-redeemer marry Ruth as part of the land exchange. When the kinsman heard this, he refused to fulfill the request. He was not willing to have Ruth bear a son and then also include that child as an heir to his property because it would decrease the amount of land that his other children stood to inherit. Immediately, Boaz stood up before the elder witnesses and expressed his desire to fulfill the role of the kinsman-redeemer and take Ruth as his wife.

As word of this agreement spread, the community rejoiced for Ruth and prayed that God would bless their marriage with children. A year later, Ruth bore a son named Obed. Naomi's friends celebrated the birth of her grandson because she could see that God had not forgotten her family. Obed grew to be a great and wealthy man, whose offspring included Jesse, the father of David, one of the greatest kings to ever rule over Israel. Through the book of Ruth, we see how God granted two women a second chance at happiness. Naomi was a broken older woman. She had experienced life at its best and also tasted of its bitterness. Yet, in her despair, she returned to God. Many times, when things do not go the way we think they should, we push away from God. We don't read the Bible; we stop praying and going to church. Much like Naomi, we too feel like God has turned against us. If you are going through a difficult situation, it is time to return to God. He alone can give you the comfort and peace that you seek. He can fill the emptiness that you feel in your heart.

Remember, Naomi did not travel back to Bethlehem alone. She had spent her life being kind and pleasant. This drew Ruth's heart toward her. When we win people's hearts, through love, we can lead them to Jesus. Both women had problems, yet they found strength in each other. When we face troubles, we cannot isolate ourselves. God will surround us with people who can travel alongside us. Naomi needed Ruth, just as much as Ruth needed her. We also see that when they returned to Bethlehem, Naomi determined to invest her energy into finding Ruth a suitable man with whom she could build a home. She wanted things to be well for Ruth. When we study that phrase, "that it may be well;" we find it means to prosper. Ruth had left everything behind and worked diligently to care for Naomi. Now, it was time for Naomi to impart wisdom into Ruth's life. Naomi's insight elevated Ruth from a poverty-stricken foreigner into a wealthy, happily married woman.

As Naomi sought what was best for Ruth, her sadness, grief, and bitterness began to leave. We cannot feel sorry for ourselves; while at the same time being preoccupied with helping others. Naomi shifted her focus from herself and made it her mission to help Ruth find true love. She became a mentor and offered counsel as she saw the hand of God moving in Ruth's life. There are young people today that desperately need your insight. They need to be loved, taught and looked after. You can draw them to you by opening your heart and sharing your story. Your life doesn't have to be perfect. All that you need is a loving, insightful heart. You have the life experience that can catapult a young person into a state of purpose and prosperity. Naomi spoke words of instruction that resulted in Ruth becoming part of the lineage that Jesus, the Messiah, was born into. She became the great-grandmother of King David. The birth of Naomi's grandson Obed caused a great celebration.

His birth marked a new season in the lives of three lonely people: Boaz, Ruth, and Naomi. They were all destined to have a second chance. When we obey God others will see His hand move in our lives. Boaz was a good husband for Ruth, but he was also a restorer of life for Naomi. Boaz represented God as our redeemer. He saw our poor, lost condition and sent Jesus to turn our sorrows into joy. We were once outcasts and exiled from God, because of sin. We were spiritually bankrupt, but Jesus paid the price for our redemption. He took us out of poverty, and we are now hidden under the wings of the almighty God. Under his shawl of grace, we are protected, provided for and loved. He can take the bitterness out of our life and restore laughter and joy into our lives. Don't allow the enemy to keep you from investing in the lives of others. Just like Naomi, God can fill the later years of your life with happiness and fulfillment. In the next chapter, we are going to continue to see how showing kindness to others always releases favor back to us.

Chapter 8

Releasing the Law of Kindness

*"She openeth her mouth with wisdom;
and in her tongue is the law of kindness."*
Proverbs 31:26

WE ARE SURROUNDED BY physical, natural, and supernatural laws. Examples of these laws include the law of gravity; what goes up must come down. The law of attraction denotes that you will attract or bring into your life those things which most consume your thoughts. In this chapter, we are going to examine the power of releasing the Law of Kindness in your life. It is a spiritual law that is rarely taught but is a powerful force that when applied can change the course of your life.

The first time that I came across this law was in Proverbs 31. This phrase "The Law of Kindness" caught my attention but I wasn't exactly sure what it was or how to apply it. I also noticed that this Virtuous Woman opens her mouth with wisdom. The Law of Kindness governs her mouth. It is the filter through which everything she speaks must flow through. We live in a time where people are rude and quick to anger. It seems as though common courtesy is an old-fashioned thing. As you look on many social media outlets, it is easy to see how people unleash mean and vindictive words, without any thought to how it might hurt someone. There is a callousness that has swept our society and people now boast about the fact that they "just tell it like it is." In other words, I am not going to filter my thinking, my words and just lash out with my tongue, regardless of any of the consequences. People can hide behind the anonymity of the internet and hurl flaming, hurtful words, without anyone knowing who they are. These words can destroy marriages, families, and have even claimed the lives of teenagers who committed suicide, because of bullying and being victimized by verbal cruelty. Our world is clamoring and crying out for genuine kindness.

A virtuous woman is one who allows the Law of Kindness to govern all of her relationships. It is easy to be nice to people with whom we interact occasionally, but the true measure of our character is what is seen by those within our own home. Do we speak words of kindness to those closest to us; our spouse, children, family members? Let's be real at home. We must allow God's love to reflect through words of kindness to our children and spouses. When they understand how much we love them, they will open their hearts to receive words of instruction and guidance.

Another area where we can release the Law of Kindness is in our vocation. When you go to work- show up with a smile. Don't hide in your cubicle without interacting with others. Allow the Law of Kindness to operate through you, because it is one of the characteristics that most reflects our Father, God. It is as powerful as the law of gravity in the way it pulls people to you. When they open up their hearts and lives to you, then you can begin to impart God's love. Always remember that hurting people tend to hurt others. They will always complain, and nothing is ever right. They will use words to cut and find fault because they hurt. When we ask God for wisdom, He will reveal their source of pain and you can share His Word to bring healing into their lives. God is looking for people, in every sector of the marketplace, who are willing to reflect His kindness and bring healing to others. He wants to draw others by reproducing His character in us.

Before we continue any further, let's discuss what kindness is not. Kindness does not mean that you allow people to walk over you. Kindness does not mean that you stay in physically, mentally, or emotionally abusive relationships. Kindness is not turning a blind eye to bad behavior, to avoid confrontation. But rather, kindness will call out wrong behavior, because you care about an individual and you truly want what is best for them. Through the Law of Kindness, you will filter your words and the tone in which you speak to them and will not be harsh or belittling. Whenever you are trying to decide whether to confront a person or not, remember to gauge your motive based on the Law of Kindness and love. Is what you are going to say truthfully? If it is truthful, is it necessary? Yes, there are times when something is true, but it does not need to be said, because it will not correct, build-up, or encourage another. Many times, people will speak something, because, "Someone has to tell them;" regardless of the consequences. These people are usually the ones who "have to tell" the pastor how to run the church. They "have to tell" the boss how to run the department. If you let them, they'll even "have to tell" you how to dress and fix your hair.

Kindness is more than just being nice. It means that you are a person of compassion. As a person of compassion, when you hear that someone is in need, you take action. The Bible tells us that Jesus was moved with compassion. That compassion led Him to feed multitudes, heal the sick, and even cry with those who mourned. Compassion will not allow you to know that someone is in need and do nothing about it. Kindness and compassion go hand-in-hand and they require us to roll up our sleeves and get involved with helping others.

Being kind and being nice are two different things. The Bible describes kindness as long-suffering. In other words, it is sustained; regardless of if it is ever reciprocated. A person who is longsuffering is one who can walk in self-restraint when they are pushed into anger. They are patient and do not immediately fly off the handle when circumstances or people come against them. Anyone can be nice to someone for a day. Anyone can be nice to people that like them and are nice to them. Kindness is beyond that because it is extended to others; regardless of what they do to us. This is where we truly imitate our Father, God. When we walk in the spirit of humbleness, kindness, and longsuffering, we draw people to God, because it is His nature.

"Put on therefore, as the elect of God, holy and beloved, bowels of mercies, kindness, humbleness of mind, meekness, longsuffering; forbearing one another, and forgiving one another, if any man have a quarrel against any: even as Christ forgave you, so also do ye." Colossians 3:12-13

These scriptures challenge us to put on kindness. It is not something we just "feel." We determine to walk in the Law of Kindness toward others because Christ forgave us. Putting on kindness requires us to yield our will and decide to forgive others. These are all choices that we make daily. The reason that we do this is, that Christ first loved us. He first forgave us. Therefore, if Christ forgave us, then he is calling us to extend that same forgiveness, kindness, and mercy to those around us. In 2 Samuel 9, we find the best example of the Law of Kindness in operation. King David is in his palace reflecting upon his life, when he remembers his best friend, Jonathan. He immediately asks his servants to find out if he has any surviving descendants. The reason David is asking is, **"That I may show him kindness for Jonathan's sake. " 2 Samuel 9:1**

Just like David, we must take time to reflect upon the people that God has placed in our lives, to help us succeed. It is good to stop and thank them for caring for us and acknowledge how their efforts have led us closer to God. As I reflect upon my own life, I think about the people involved in the children's ministry of Faith Tabernacle in Defiance, Ohio. I was a little girl, about six years old when they would send a church bus out to our little country house to pick up my brother and me and take us to Sunday school. I loved going to church because the people were nice, and it was a fun place to go. I even got to do crafts! I realize now, how much these people loved God and how they planted the Word in my little heart. You see, what I didn't know then, is that even though my mind only had the comprehension level of a six-year-old child, my spirit is eternal and does not have an age. Therefore, as these teachers taught me stories from the Bible, faith seeds were being planted in my heart. **"So then, Faith comes by hearing, and hearing by the Word of God." Romans 10:17**

They were not just babysitting a bunch of kids. They were people who God placed in my path to draw me to him. My parents did not attend church regularly and my father was addicted to drugs and alcohol. I knew that he loved us, but because of his addictions, my parents fought constantly. I saw how he abused my mother and I lived in fear of making him angry because I didn't want to be spanked. Then, one day, the Holy Spirit used me, a little first-grader, to speak to my father, and God convicted him of his sin. That was the beginning of my father's miraculous transformation. He was set free from heroin, alcohol, and drugs. Today, my father is a minister of the gospel and travels all over South Texas, preaching how Jesus Christ can set anyone free from bondage. I thank God for those people at Sunday School. If not for them, I could very well have been just another statistic; a high school dropout and unwed, teenage mother, with no education and trapped in a system of poverty.

As David reflected on his life, he remembered how Jonathan saved him. King Saul was Jonathan's father and he wanted to protect the throne for his son. During his reign, Saul disobeyed God and the prophet Samuel foretold Saul that he and his descendants would lose the throne of Israel. After David killed Goliath, the people fell in love with the brave, young shepherd boy and rallied around him. As his popularity grew, Saul quickly realized that David would one day become king, and from that moment on, he plotted to kill him. However, David and Jonathan had formed a strong friendship. Jonathan recognized that God's hand was upon David, and instead of being jealous or seeing David as an enemy, Jonathan protected him. Jonathan had a revelation that this shepherd boy would one day rule over Israel. Jonathan was a true friend and helped David escape from Saul's numerous assassination attempts. In I Samuel 20 we read about David and Jonathan's last meeting. Jonathan exposed his father's plan to murder David and he tells David to flee. But, before they part ways, the two friends renewed the covenant that they had made years before, ***"The Lord be between me and thee, and between my seed and thy seed forever." I Samuel 20:42***

That was the last time that David would ever see his friend because Jonathan was later killed in battle. The years passed and David remembered his covenant. This covenant was more than just a promise between friends. It went deeper because it was witnessed by the Lord. Covenant, in the Old Testament, meant a bond that was formed by two or more people who would each agree to fulfill the duties of the agreement. The agreement was not one-sided; each party had to do something. Now that David was king, he had the opportunity to honor his friend, by fulfilling his covenant. We too must be very careful to honor the commitments that we make to our family, friends, and those closest to us. Let us strive to be people of integrity, who can be depended upon. David said, ***"Is there yet any that is left of the house of Saul, that I may show him kindness for Jonathan's sake?" 2 Samuel 9:1***

A couple of things strike me about his question: First, is the fact that David even mentions Saul, his sworn enemy. He attempted to kill David, and yet, David still honors this man's name. I believe, it is because David respected the office that Saul held. David understood that God had anointed Saul to be king, and even when Saul walked away from God, David continued to respect the call of God that was upon Saul's life. Many times, when leaders fail or fall away from God, people are quick to judge them and talk badly about them. David understood the danger of coming against a person anointed by God. When David had the opportunity to kill Saul, he would not do it, because of the office in which God had placed Saul. I believe we should honor and respect our leaders. We should hold them in prayer before God, but if they fall or fail, it is God who will judge them. They will stand before God and give account for their actions. We must exercise wisdom and let the Law of Kindness guard the words that we speak when it comes to talking about those in leadership roles. It is a position that comes with great responsibility and much accountability.

The second point I noticed is that David intends to show kindness upon the descendants of Jonathan, because of Jonathan's sake. Nobody was aware of the covenant that existed between them, but it was written in David's heart. Jonathan's descendants did not have a legal document that they could use to demand that David provide for them. Instead, they would simply benefit from a covenant that they didn't even know existed. David would show them kindness, because of it. They did not earn it. They did not deserve it. They received it, just because they were descendants of Jonathan. Jonathan recognized that the hand of God was upon David and he aligned himself with him. This association impacted his family for generations. Saul's disobedience to God brought death and destruction to his sons. Jonathan's kindness toward David restored dignity to his family lineage. Ziba was a servant in David's court, who had also served in the palace during Saul's reign. When David sought information about Saul's household, Ziba was brought into the court and he informed the king of Jonathan's son, Mephibosheth, who was lame and lived in Lodebar.

Mephibosheth was only five years old when his grandfather, father, and uncles all died. When news of their deaths reached his nanny, she immediately fled Jerusalem with Mephibosheth, to protect him from being killed. She feared that David, or anyone else seeking to take over the throne of Saul, would kill Mephibosheth since he was the only remaining heir to the throne. As they fled in terror, she dropped Mephibosheth and he became lame. He could no longer walk. From that moment on, Mephibosheth's life was marked with fear and disappointment. He had no family and was provided for out of the kindness of Machir in Lodebar. After hearing that Mephibosheth was alive, David sent Ziba to Lodebar to bring him to the palace. Lodebar was a place of no pasture. It was a desolate, dry place west of Jerusalem. Imagine Mephibosheth's life.

He could not walk and was helpless. He knew very little about his family lineage, other than the fact that his grandfather had been the king of Israel. He probably remembered very little about his father, Jonathan, and so for all of these years, he lived in fear. People were misinformed and they told him to stay away from David. They told him that David would destroy him. Then, one day, the city began to buzz with excitement, as a beautiful caravan from the king's palace approached. Ziba arrived in front of Machir's home and sought Mephibosheth, with orders to bring him to David. Mephibosheth fled Jerusalem, with nothing, and now he was returning mounted on a royal convoy. As they approached Jerusalem, Mephibosheth's mind was flooded with fear. When they finally reached the palace, King David called his name and spoke unimaginable words. ***"Fear not; for I will surely show thee kindness for Jonathan thy father's sake, and I will restore thee all the land of Saul thy father, and though shalt eat bread at my table continually." 2 Samuel 9:7***

David told him not to fear. He said, I do not plan to hurt you; rather, I will restore what belonged to your family, because of Jonathan's sake. David was a man of honor. He did not know who Mephibosheth was. He didn't know that he even existed, but because of the covenant, David showed a blessing toward him. In that instant, Mephibosheth went from being a beggar, living from the generosity of people, to a rich landowner. In Lodebar, Mephibosheth forgot who he was. He forgot that there was royalty running through his veins. His DNA was made up of the royalty of Saul and Jonathan. David remembered the covenant and knew that it was time for Mephibosheth to have what belonged to him. It had been in David's possession for too long.

David released the Law of Kindness into Mephibosheth's life. Just like Jonathan had been kind to a young shepherd fleeing for his life, now this powerful king would be kind to his son. When Jonathan and David met, David had nothing but shepherds clothing, a sling, and five stones. Immediately after killing Goliath, Jonathan and David became friends. Jonathan gave David his royal robe, sword, bow, and girdle, not knowing that one day, his lame son would enter the palace in rags and his friend David would dress Mephibosheth in royal garments- fit for a king's table. David's kindness and love were exemplary of God's kindness. It came out of a merciful heart. He did not have to seek out Mephibosheth. Nobody even knew he was alive, except for Ziba. Nobody had memory of him.

Upon receiving such kindness, Mephibosheth bowed down and asked why David would be so kind. He considered himself to be as useless as a dead dog, but Mephibosheth, whose name meant "exterminator of shame," would experience the benefit of kindness. The shame would be lifted from his family. As a child, change happened all around him and he could not control any of it. In Lodebar, he was stripped of his identity, his prestige, his rank, and respectability. No one knew who he was, and he was hiding in obscurity, where nobody wanted him. In Lodebar, Mephibosheth lost everything. As a child, his nanny tried to protect him, but she fell and failed him. ***"Then the king called Ziba, Saul's servant, and said unto him, I have given unto they master's sons all that pertained to Saul and to all his house...but Mephibosheth thy master's son shall eat bread always at my table". 2 Samuel 9:9-10***

In an instant, Mephibosheth went from being a beggar to being a landowner. David returned Saul's land back to Mephibosheth. The Bible does not specify how much land that was, but we are told that David also assigned Ziba and his 15 sons and 20 servants to care for all of the property. Mephibosheth was moved into David's palace, and from that day forward, he ate from the king's table. He was completely provided for, because of the covenant that was enacted, based upon the Law of Kindness. ***"So Mephibosheth dwelt in Jerusalem; for he did eat continually at the king's table; and was lame on both his feet." 2 Samuel 9:13***

As Mephibosheth took his place at the king's table, he was no longer defined by his past. Yes, he was still lame in both feet, but when he took his place at the table, nobody saw his deficiency. When he was dressed in royal robes, none of the servants noticed his crippled legs, as they served the daily meals. Yes, he was handicapped, but it didn't matter when he was sitting at the king's table. He looked just like any other honored guest. Mephibosheth did nothing to receive David's kindness. He was simply the recipient of David's compassion and mercy. David was lavish in his giving toward him. David was vested in Mephibosheth's success. He gave him back everything that belonged to his family and even assigned servants to help him. God is lavish in His thoughts toward you. This is why He pours out new mercies before us, every day. We can take this Law of Kindness with us wherever we go. Today, no matter what you are facing, fear not. Fear not what people say about you. Fear not what the circumstances look like. God is going to show kindness toward you. He loves you and is for you.

Just like Mephesobeth, many people are living their lives as cripples. As a result, they are crippled by anger, guilt, despair, and depression. People failed and hurt them. They may not have meant to, but human nature is flawed and often the people closest to us feel cause the greatest pain or endure the consequences of our mistakes. The enemy wants to keep us in Lodebar, with a Lodebar mindset. A mindset that is dry and desolate. It does not allow you to produce positive results in your life. It is only thinking about lack, fear, pain, and regret. You may have been dropped by people. They may have left you and hurt you in Lodebar. Now, you live with a scar. There is a wound and it hurts. Today, you are facing a decision. Do you stay in Lodebar or are you ready to sit at the king's table? God sees your imperfections. He sees how people have failed you, but the past does not matter. He doesn't care about your mistakes, the abortion, the divorce, or anything else. He wants you to take your place at His table. You are redeemed from guilt and condemnation.

Today is your day to get out of Lodebar. God has sent the Holy Spirit to draw you to Him and seat you where you belong. In Psalms 23 David wrote, "He prepareth a table before you in the presence of your enemies". God wants to seat you at the table of His provision and protection. Shame, anger, bitterness are all enemies that keep you from truly enjoying your life. It is time to dust off the shame. Leave the past behind you, because your future is promising. It does not matter who has disappointed you or failed you. God wants to restore everything. Whatever situation you are facing today, God can supply an answer. If you are facing sickness, He can heal. If you need a job, God has one for you. If you need deliverance from addiction, the power of Jesus' name can set you free. If you need peace for your mind, Jesus can restore your soul. God wants to lift you. His Loving-Kindness is reaching out to you so that you can step out of despair and sit with Him.

Today just like Mephesobeth, we are the beneficiaries of a covenant our faith father Abraham made. We were all lost and were not even thinking about a relationship with God. We did not even know anything about the impact of covenants. But God was mindful of the covenant He made with Abraham. Remember, what God said to Abraham in chapter 3? He told Abraham to leave out of Ur and go to an unknown place and by faith, "through you, all the people of the earth will be blessed? "Abraham obeyed God and God allowed him to see into the future to the day our redeemer Jesus would come. Jesus said in John 8:56 "Your father Abraham rejoiced to see my day: and he saw it, and was glad." You too can rejoice in knowing that God's loving-kindness is working on your behalf.

Chapter 9

Experience Brings Hope

Favour is deceitful, and beauty is vain: but a woman that feareth the LORD, she shall be praised.
Proverbs 31:30

THIS ENDING VERSE OF Proverbs 31 is a celebration of a life well-lived. At the beginning of the chapter, Solomon described a rare virtuous young woman. We saw her evolve from a young bride into a mother, working with her husband to provide for their children. She had her own business and used her means to help the poor. She skillfully managed the resources within her home, and she conducted herself with dignity. Solomon concludes the chapter with a call for her family and community to praise her for her good works. We see that Solomon points out that she was able to live honorably because she feared the Lord. What made this virtuous woman remarkable is that she trusted God throughout her entire life. Many people struggle with aging and will go to extremes to try and look younger. But, in this chapter, we see that beauty and our appearance is fleeting. This virtuous woman kept the right focus, developing her relationship with God throughout her entire life.

In Proverbs 9:10 Solomon writes that "the beginning of wisdom, is the fear of the Lord." This is not the kind of fear that is afraid of God in that sense that God is going to punish or strike a person down with lightning. Instead, it is to respect God as you would a person that you esteem and trust. When we worship God, his Holy Spirit will lead and instruct us in every area of our life. His Holy Spirit will help you understand the Bible and find peace during the difficult circumstances of life. This is why in Proverbs 31:25 the virtuous woman was not fearful. She was clothed in God's presence and would not fear the future but was confident. We are told she shall rejoice in time to come.

This confidence or dependence on God was developed over time. In Romans 5:1-5 the progression of hope is defined: **Romans 5 Therefore being justified by faith, we have peace with God through our Lord Jesus Christ:2 By whom also we have access by faith into this grace wherein we stand, and rejoice in hope of the glory of God. And not only so, but we glory in tribulations also: knowing that tribulation worketh patience; And patience, experience; and experience, hope: And hope maketh not ashamed; because the love of God is shed abroad in our hearts by the Holy Ghost which is given unto us.**

In this book, we looked at the lives of ordinary people that overcame impossible situations. Yet they each had one thing in common, they obtained a right relationship with God through faith. Sin separates people from God. It condemns them to spiritual death. Sin points out the fact that they have failed a perfectly holy God. However, faith in

Jesus restores a relationship with God. That relationship with God gave the believers in this book peace regardless of the difficulties they faced. God's peace opened their spiritual eyes to see that no matter what they faced; they were not alone. As believers in Christ, we are at peace with God. Faith in Jesus grants us access to the very throne of God. We can go to Him with any situation in full confidence that we are forgiven, and He is listening to our prayers. This hope is not wishful thinking for a better tomorrow. It is a confident, assurance that after this life, we will be in heaven in the glory and very presence of God. Heaven is a real place that God has prepared for those that believe in Him and trust in His Son Jesus Christ. This belief does not exempt us from problems on earth. Romans 5:3 states that ***we glory in tribulations also*** Why?

Tribulations reveal our beliefs. Tribulations expose the fears, uncertainties, and doubts we carry and force us to trust in God. The challenges we face in life do not prove anything to God. He already knows our heart, intentions, and motives. They are a mirror that reflects our inner man, our thinking and what we truly believe. Tribulations strengthen our relationship with God because we understand that when we face challenges and disappointments something is being produced in us. Tribulations produce patience. Another word for patience is endurance. Our faith in God remains strong regardless of what is happening around us. It took Abraham and Sarah twenty-five years to finally have their son and during that period, Abraham continued to believe that God would fulfill his promise. As he waited on God, he developed endurance. Our timing for when we want God to answer is not always the same as God's. However, we later see that when He brings things into completion, they are perfect. As we see God's hand move in our lives, we start to depend and hope on Him in greater dimensions. We reflect and see how He helped us through a particular situation and know that if He was with us then, He will continue to lead us. These are beautiful experiences that increase our faith and dependence on God. This is the progression that the Apostle Paul wrote about in Romans. Tribulations produce patience, patience brings experience and experience cultivates hope.

The virtuous woman walked with God throughout her life. She saw how God was with her and her family and this is why she could look at the future and rejoice. She had true hope and was confident that all would be well. Biblical hope is not the same as natural hope. Biblical hope is based on the truth of God's word. It is based on a relationship with a God that cannot fail us. Natural hope is wishful thinking that is based on the desired outcome. It is like building your house on sand when the tide rolls in, the foundation is washed away. We have placed our hope on Jesus the Rock which is certain. Allow His Spirit to guide you today. Seek His leading for whatever situation you are going through. His love will wipe away your tears. If you are grieving the loss of a loved one, know that they are rejoicing in His presence. There is hope that you will see them again. Our hope is based on the love of God that made a way for us to be united with Him in eternity. His love for us is so great that we cannot even grasp or comprehend what eternity really means but He is guiding us there.

When we look through God's eyes we look to the future with anticipation and full expectancy that His plans and purposes will be completed in our lives. In Jeremiah 29:11 he tells us that ***"I know the thoughts that I think toward*** *you, saith the LORD, thoughts of peace, and not of evil, to give you an expected end."* This verse brings me so much joy, to know that God has thoughts of peace, and not evil for me and there is an expected end to my life. He has a course for us to run and we can run it confidently. Just like the cross-country runners, the terrain may be rocky and sometimes it's uphill but we can each complete the course. This world is becoming increasingly violent, antagonistic towards Christianity but as believers, we can be assured that God is with us. David was being hunted down to be killed by King Saul and yet he wrote this *Psalm.121:1-2 "I will lift up mine eyes unto the hills, from whence cometh my help. My help cometh from the Lord, which made heaven and earth. He will not suffer thy foot to be moved. "*

We too lift our eyes and look to God. When we look up we can be assured that He will be with us as we face the future. When we look up strength comes to us. This trust brings us the strength to take a stand against evil. It gives us the confidence to know He hears and answers our prayers. We are not alone. Our future is in His hands. Look to the Future and Laugh!

Chapter 10

Call Her Blessed

*Her children arise up, and call her blessed;
her husband also, and he praiseth her.*
Proverbs 31:28

LAST YEAR, I HAD THE opportunity to spend some time with a woman that had been diagnosed with breast cancer. The doctor's report stunned her. She had experienced no symptoms, so this report was the last thing she expected to hear. She told me that when they gave her the diagnosis, she responded by saying, "*No. This is not going to stop me. My grand-daughters are graduating next year and I'm going to be there.*" As I looked at her, I was amazed at the faith and resistance with which she was fighting this battle. She proceeded to tell me everything that God had done in her life and she was confident He was going to take her through this valley as well. This is her story.

My friend was born in south Texas to a hard-working housekeeper. They were poor but her mother was a beautiful and proud woman. She watched her mother come home tired from work and she promised herself that she would never become a housekeeper. Her goal was to one day work in an office as a secretary. Like any young woman her age, she was full of hope and energy. She loved to dance and have fun with her friends. It was at a dancehall where she met a young man who swept her off her feet. She was there with her friends when they met, and he asked her to dance. Immediately she was drawn to him. They dated, fell in love, and talked about getting married someday. However, all of that changed the moment she found out she was pregnant. She knew she would have to tell her parents. When her mother heard the news; she was shocked, angry, and disappointed. It was the sixties and to be pregnant out of wedlock was very shameful. People looked down on unwed mothers, judging them and their families. My friend was confronted by the pressure of having an abortion. She thought it would be the easiest way to cope with this situation. This would allow her time to finish her schooling, get rid of the "loser" boyfriend, and also keep the family's good reputation. No one would ever know about this pregnancy.

As the day got closer for my friend to have an abortion, she felt so confused. She loved her boyfriend and she knew he loved her too. But she was also torn because she never wanted to shame her family, it just happened. Now she was faced with the biggest decision of her life. Would she listen to other people and have the abortion, or would she have this baby? She prayed, cried, and felt all alone. There was no one to turn to. She decided to have an abortion. The year was 1967, abortions were not legal. As they pulled into the driveway, her heart raced, and she knew that she could not go through with it. In an act of courage, she refused to go through with the abortion. She didn't care what the future would bring or what people would say. You see the courageous woman is she is not only my friend, but she is also my mother. She loved me and knew that I was not a mistake. She felt that even if she had to raise me by herself, she would find a way to take care of us. But she didn't have to because when my father found out that my mother was pregnant, they immediately got married.

Their marriage had a rocky start. They were both very young and dad did the best he could do to provide for his new bride and baby girl working as a migrant. They followed the crops and travel whether they could find work. They went to Northwest Ohio to harvest the tomato crops when dad heard that General Motors was hiring. He had an uncle that worked at the plant and he was able to help my father get hired. Taking the job was a difficult decision because they would be thousands of miles away from their family, but they were willing to do it. This job would provide a stable income, they would no longer be migrants and it would give them a better future for their children. Finally, it seemed like their "luck" had changed.

At first, everything seemed to be going fine. But eventually, my father started abusing drugs and alcohol. My father is a gifted musician so for fun, he played the accordion in a Spanish Tejano band. I can still remember watching him get ready to go out and play at one of his gigs. I was about five years old and I would beg him not to leave. I would stand in front of our front door with my arms spread wide trying to block the door, pleading, "Daddy don't go." He would simply push me aside and walk out. We lived in a tiny run-down house out in the country. When he would leave mom and I would hold each other and cry. The reason we cried was that we never knew what to expect when daddy came back home. Sometimes he would come home and start fighting and screaming at my mother accusing her of cheating on him, which was not even possible. Mom was isolated. She had no friends, no job, no car, no money and no family there for her. All she had was me and my little brother. Other times, he would come home high and could barely move. This pattern of abuse and chaos continued week after week. Every Saturday night, mother and I would sit and cry waiting for dad to come home. I knew my dad loved us but he was bound to drugs and alcohol. He was able to keep his job but he spent all of the money on his addictions.

One day, the phone rang and I answered. It was another woman asking for my father. As a little girl, I didn't think anything of it and just shouted out. "Daddy your girlfriend wants to talk to you." Well, that didn't go over to good and before I knew it, my mother, brother and I were on our way to my grandmother's house in Texas. It was near the end of fall and my paternal grandparents were finishing the tomato season in Ohio. They packed up the harvest truck with their few belongings. My mom, my brother, and I along with several family members rode in the back of that old canvas-covered harvest truck all the way to South Texas. After a few months of separation, my parents decide to reconcile. Mom was scared of returning to Ohio but she was willing to take a chance again because she loved my dad and wanted us to be a family. At first, things seemed to be better, but she soon found herself back in a pattern of abuse. Dad was having an affair and she was completely alone. Her family had warned her not to go back so now she had no one to turn to. Just when she thought she had made the biggest mistake of her life, God stepped in.

He sent people who began to speak into my father's life and explain that God could set him free from his addictions and give him a new start. God even spoke to my father through me. I remember going to church one Sunday morning on the church bus. As I was getting off the bus, they told us to bring our parents to church later that evening because there was going to be a special speaker. I didn't know what they meant I just wanted to go to church because it was fun and peaceful there. People loved me. So, I ran into the house and asked my parents to take us back to church. My father said no because he had planned a surprise for us. We were going to the movies. Well, that was a big deal for us. We never went to the movies. The movie he was taking us to was a Spanish cowboy movie in a little theater. We all sat watching the movie when all of a sudden, they began to show some sexually explicit scenes. At that moment, my father felt convicted. He later testified that he heard a voice speaking inside of him. "***Your daughter asked you to take your family to church and you refused. You'd rather your children see this than learn about me?***"

My father was furious and grabbed all of us and we stormed out of the movie theater. He forced us all into the car and drove to buy a six-pack of beer. I had no idea what was happening. I just knew my dad was very angry cussing up a storm and driving recklessly. I was frightened and began weeping uncontrollably. My father asked me why I was crying. I couldn't explain it, I was just scared. I was afraid of him, afraid of getting into trouble and afraid of being beaten by him. After he promised not to spank me, the Holy Spirit spoke through me. When he once again asked me why

I was crying, I replied "Daddy, you're not hurting anybody. You're just hurting yourself and you're hurting Jesus." Instantly, my dad threw out the beer he was drinking and realized he needed to turn his life over to God. My dad began crying and promised us that he was going to change. He accepted Jesus Christ as his Savior. That day was the day our family legacy changed.

My mother began to see how God was transforming my dad's life. She saw how he was instantaneously, miraculously freed from his heroin addiction. She noticed how he would spend hours reading the Bible and trying to learn more about God. She felt this was all good for him because he was a really bad sinner and needed to change, but my mother didn't think she needed all of that for herself. My mother was a religious woman and did not hurt anyone. She was a homemaker who did her best to take care of her husband and her three children. Then one day, God spoke to her heart. Not in a loud audible voice but in her spirit. The Holy Spirit began to show my mother how she too was a sinner because even though my dad was changing, mom had bitterness and unforgiveness in her heart towards him because of the years of abuse she had endured.

She resented the woman with whom my dad had an affair with. She took out her frustrations on my brother and me and would spank us in anger. The Holy Spirit showed her the hidden areas of her heart so that she could see that she also needed to accept Jesus as her Savior and ask Him to forgive her. It had been easy to justify herself when she compared her past to my father's past. However, when she saw her heart condition compared to the purity of Jesus' love and God's measure of perfection, she realized she too needed to accept Jesus. That decision changed our home.

My parents have been married for almost fifty years now. Through the years they have seen God's hand upon their children and their grandchildren. God has opened doors for them to travel throughout the small border towns of South Texas proclaiming the Good news of the gospel. They have shared their testimony with thousands of people and have led them to Jesus Christ.

I call my mother blessed not because she's perfect. I call her blessed because she fears the Lord. She lives her life supporting her husband and following the call of God upon their lives. Their passion in life is to lead other young families to Jesus everywhere they go. Through the years my mother has faced many of the same challenges confronted by the women we have studied throughout this book. She has experienced the loss of close family members, stood beside me in faith, and encouraged me to believe I would have a child as I went through the years of infertility. She had to let go of the bitterness, anger, and unforgiveness that she felt towards my dad to save her marriage. She had to allow God to rebuild it. As they've shared their story of salvation and restoration, God has intervened in the lives of many young marriages. God took their pain and made it their platform.

You see this is what it means to be a Virtuous Woman. It means we walk out our faith and trust in the Lord through every season of life. We don't just one day arrive at this super-spiritual place in God. A Virtuous Woman is one that faces every challenge in life through the lens of faith. This is why she can look at the future and laugh. Her eyes are fixed on what God says about the circumstance.

No matter where you are today, you can have a new beginning in your walk with the Lord. If the past has been one of pain and disappointment, today is the day you can release it. The love of God can set you free from the bondages of shame, guilt, anger, confusion or anything else you feel. Your life has a purpose. You were created in the image of God and He has a plan for you. Others may have told you that you were a mistake, but that is a lie. Life is a precious gift and it really is simple to have a fresh start. All you have to do is ask Jesus to forgive you of the past and make Him Lord of your life. In other words, you surrender your way of doing things and begin to seek His way of living. As you do this day by day, His word will shift your focus from this limited natural view to His supernatural perspective. You will be able to look to the future with hope and expectation. You will be able to laugh because you know that God is faithful and that He has already given you the victory through His Son Jesus Christ.

Epilogue

MY FATHER ENTERED heaven on July 8, 2019. I am proud to say that my father dedicated his life to the call of the Evangelist. He and my mother, Oralia spent over 40 years together ministering to the downcast, burdened, drug addicts, and broken-hearted. He fully understood the ministry of "presence."

Dad was frequently called upon to officiate funeral services of anyone in need. He brought comfort to the grieving. He boldly proclaimed the power and hope that is found in the resurrection of Jesus Christ. His greatest joy was setting up his gospel tent in his hometown of Robstown, TX, and the poorest cities along the U.S and Mexico borders. There my parents would share the good news of the Gospel and deliver a message of hope. It was through this ministry that marriages were reconciled, drug addicts were set free and lives were restored.

My father's last words to me were, "God is going to open up nations and platforms to you to reach hundreds for Jesus."

Dad, thank you for being such a wonderful example of a "workman of the Lord Jesus Christ not ashamed, rightly dividing the word of truth." You were bold, loving and a truly awesome man of God! Until we are reunited in glory, I will continue carrying forward the cause of Christ.

Therefore, my beloved brethren, be steadfast, immovable, always abounding in the work of the Lord, knowing that your labor is not in vain in the Lord.
I Corinthians 15:58

About the Author

ANNA HERNANDEZ is a speaker, teacher, and businesswoman. She and her husband, George travel throughout the United States encouraging audiences to discover their unique talents and abilities to make a difference in the marketplace. Together, they have established Eternal Impact Media Ministries which continues to carry on her father's legacy of reaching lost people, teaching and equipping believers, helping families become Christlike, and preparing leaders for the work of the ministry.

Anna is a skilled business strategist with over 25 years of corporate marketing and sales experience. Her passion is helping people turn their talents into viable businesses that bring God's light into the marketplace. She is a graduate of Agape Faith Bible Training Center, Birch, Run Michigan, and holds a B.A. in Marketing Management.

Contact Information

ANNA CAN BE CONTACTED:
Eternalimpact@live.com
989-737-1334
Facebook: Eternal Impact Media Ministries